Matters of Faith and Matters of Principle

Religious Truth Claims and Their Logic

Matters of Faith and Matters of Principle

Religious Truth Claims and Their Logic

John H. Whittaker

Trinity University Press   San Antonio

for
C.H.W., R.E.W., Sr.
and
C.B.W.

CONTENTS

PREFACE

Anything which one says about religious belief is likely to sound suspicious, and anything which one presents as a *logical* analysis is apt to sound doubly suspicious, as if some religious claims were about to be upheld or condemned in the name of "logic." But that is not what I have in mind. My aim in these essays is more general and more modest than that. By clarifying the logic of religious assertions, I simply want to show that a reasonable religious belief is a logical *possibility:* matters of faith need not be arbitrary matters of taste and temperament.

Making this point, though, turns out to be surprisingly difficult. Religious assertions can almost never be confirmed or disconfirmed; they resist every objectively compelling form of rational justification, forcing believers to hold their convictions "by faith." If believers had no alternatives in such matters, this resort to faith might not be so troublesome. Given the many religious and secular alternatives held out to us, however, one wonders what, if anything, entitles believers to their particular convictions. Proof, evidently, is too much to expect for religious claims. Yet what can we expect? Empirical evidence? Inner illumination? Practical confirmation? Or is the demand for justification simply inappropriate? Perhaps *grounds* for belief are not required in such matters because *truth* is not really at stake.

All of these options, I think, are too crudely defined to fit the peculiar logic of faith. Instead of choosing among them I have tried to develop another approach, not by inventing a new category of logical analysis but by refurbishing an old one. My thesis is that religious beliefs typically play the role of principles, indemonstrable assertions which ground and condition further judgment. Religious language includes more than statements of principles, of course; some religious utterances are not *assertions* at all, while other religious claims are essentially historical or moral judgments. I am not interested in cataloging all the various types of religious language, however. Instead of that more comprehensive task, I merely want to add a new entry to the list of possible headings here, so that the most crucial doctrines of religion—its minimum articles of faith—can be classified more accurately as matters of principle. Once this is accomplished, religious teachings begin to look much less peculiar, and a little more credible, than they have in a long time.

Several prominent philosophers of religion were patient enough to read rough drafts of these essays, and I would like to thank them for their willing response and constructive criticism. Paul Holmer, William Christian, Norman Malcolm, Alastair McKinnon, D. Z. Phillips, Robert Ayers, W. D. Hudson, Jude Dougherty, and David Little all offered encouragement and advice. When I had done my best to strengthen my arguments, John Hayes and Lois Boyd, editors, and Susan Owen, typist, offered valuable help in improving my style.

JOHN H. WHITTAKER
Batesville, Virginia

Matters of Faith and Matters of Principle

Religious Truth Claims
and Their Logic

I
ON CERTAINTY,
FAITH, AND DOUBT

When moved by faith, religious believers sometimes speak with certainty about such things as the existence of God; when moved by the rigorous logic of a "proof," philosophers sometimes agree. Yet most of us realize that religious beliefs never quite escape the worrisome possibility of doubt. Believers who feel certain give us only their testimony, never compelling reasons for belief, and the arguments of the philosophers remain strangely academic, applicable only to the lifeless "God of the philosophers." Thus we know at heart that religious beliefs are not certainties. They will never convert to the kind of public knowledge which everyone takes for granted, and we need not expect them to. In religious matters—matters of *faith*—one can never simply *settle* the truth and be done with it.

Few philosophers would disagree with this; the indemonstrable character of religious beliefs is just too obvious. Yet the reason for this characteristic feature of religious claims is not so obvious. The most natural explanation is that we are confined to *belief* in matters of faith because we are not in a position to *know*. In logical terms, this suggests that religious assertions are *hypotheses*—i.e., uncertain propositions whose truth or falsity might in principle, if not in practice, be established by some kind of factual inquiry. Until we have all the facts we need, we cannot determine the truth of such beliefs; so we have to weigh our reasons for belief against our reasons for doubt. The only unusual thing about religious beliefs in this respect seems to be the extraordinary difficulty of assembling a compelling amount of evidence. Such evidence is not only hard to gather but hard to conceive. Perhaps it is available in some other supramundane dimension of experience, in an afterlife or in a private world of inner experience; but in this world, where our convictions are formed, the evidence that we have for religious claims is never enough to transform faith into knowledge.

To treat religious beliefs as hypotheses, therefore, makes affirmations of faith look like guesswork. The believer adopts an unconfirmed hypothesis in the hope that the missing evidence, when it finally becomes available, will bear out his judgment, meanwhile hedging his bet as best he can. It takes only a moment's reflection, though, to see that there is something wrong with this view of religious belief. Aside from difficulties of explaining how religious claims might be verified by non-empirical, nonobjective evidence, this view of faith confuses it with conjecture. Wherever conjectures are called for, the reasonable believer proportions his beliefs to the available evidence; if this evidence is thin, he remains all the more tentative in his judgments. He avoids all undue risks by severely limiting the extent to which he *acts* on his conjectures. Wherever religious questions are at issue, however, the adoption of a belief is far more consequential. Those who affirm a religious truth are expected not only to act on it but to conform inwardly to it in their disposition, in their outlook on life, and in their self-understanding. Without relating to religious beliefs in this way, belief itself remains incomplete. The profession of belief rings hollow, and faith degenerates into mere assent.

Thus, if the reasonable *religious* believer is bound to limit the degree of his commitment to the degree of supporting evidence available for his beliefs, one who thoroughly commits himself to his religious beliefs must be judged to be unreasonable. If he ignores a due sense of proportion between his grounds and his practice, resting the heaviest concerns of his life on unsettled hypotheses, he is bound to seem excessive. Evidence generally runs low in religious controversies, but personal involvement runs high, and this disproportion makes affirmations of faith seem like perilous leaps, as if the believer were risking his life on the basis of mere speculation.

Yet a faithful adherence to religious teachings may be more appropriate than tentative assent, despite the notorious difficulty of justifying these claims. For religious beliefs need not be construed as hypotheses, and the rational ideals which apply to conjectures do not have to apply to faith claims. Religious assertions may be truth claims of an entirely different sort, not hypotheses to be tested and confirmed by the measure of factual evidence but truths to live by — truths which must prove themselves somehow in practice. The role which these beliefs play in the thinking and living of believers may be more pertinent to their credibility than anything else, and believers who abide by them without being able to defend them on logical grounds may not be as unreasonable as they seem. The regulative significance of religious assertions, in other words, might be their most definitive logical feature, and their power to transform a believer's life may have more to do with the resolution of his doubts than the collection of evidence.

The only trouble with this idea is that the believer cannot conform to his beliefs without thinking that these beliefs are *true to begin with.* The practical significance which these beliefs acquires as regulative assertions, as truths to live by, does not disarm the question of their truth; it compounds it. Those who are troubled by religious questions and uncertain about their beliefs need assurances of some kind to answer their doubts, and the knowledge that the very shape of their lives and the pattern of their thoughts turn on these issues only aggravates the problem. Where are the assurances to come from? If evidence or independent grounds for religious belief cannot overcome the potential believer's doubts, what else could? How else could any belief be reasonably held?

Such questions make the tendency to treat religious beliefs

as hypotheses almost irresistible. Religious assertions, it seems, must first prove themselves as truths before they can be reasonably affirmed as truths to live by. For that some independent measure of their truth is needed, something which has nothing to do with the practical aspects of believing — i.e., something like evidence. There seems to be no other alternative. If religious beliefs are not defensible, at least in principle, as hypotheses, it is hard to see how they might be reasonably affirmed as truths.

Yet the ideal notion that every reasonable truth claim must be grounded in evidence of some kind cannot possibly apply to all our beliefs. Some beliefs, as Ludwig Wittgenstein showed, lie so deeply ingrained in our thinking that it does not make sense to doubt them.[1] They neither need nor permit the kind of justification which hypotheses require because their truth is as certain as anything which could be advanced in their support. Reasonable people take such beliefs — "certainties," as Wittgenstein called them — for granted, not because they independently have verified their truth but because their understanding of what it means to think critically entails acting in conformity with them. Believing and behaving actually coalesce on the level of these certainties, so that one cannot proceed with rational inquiries without relying on the truth of these beliefs.

Beliefs like that are not hypotheses. When the connection between believing and behaving is so close that one's understanding of reasonable thinking depends on the acceptance of certain beliefs, the beliefs in question can no longer be adjudicated on independent grounds. The reasonableness of such beliefs is not a function of evidence but of quite different considerations, none of which can be translated into convincing arguments for their truth.

Wittgenstein was thinking only marginally about religious beliefs when he made this observation about the non-hypothetical nature of our most entrenched beliefs. The beliefs that he had in mind, unlike religious claims, were the sort that we all might agree in describing as certainties. Yet this observation contributes more to the resolution of reason and faith controversies than any other aspect of his work, even more than his lectures on religious belief.[2] The lectures call attention to the regulative role of religious beliefs, emphasizing the disparity in understanding between skeptics, who treat such beliefs as unreasonable hypotheses, and believers, who conform their thoughts to them as truths to live by. How this regulative role of religious beliefs affects their rational justification, however, remains obscure. This air of obscurity does not begin to clear up until the peculiar features of religious assertions are brought within the larger logical compass of the notes *On Certainty*. Religious beliefs, of course, are hardly certainties, but if certainties can be reasonably believed without being justified on prior logical grounds, perhaps the same might be said of religious claims. Perhaps the possibility of a reasonable faith has little or nothing to do with the defense of hypotheses. That is what Wittgenstein's remarks on certainties and on religious beliefs suggest.

Wittgenstein himself never elaborated the point, and so those who would pursue this suggestion must do so on their own. The place to start, however, is with Wittgenstein's treatment of philosophical skepticism; for his defense of commonsensical beliefs in the face of philosophical doubts invites a similar view of religious beliefs and religious doubts. The comparison is too simple to sustain in any final analysis of religious truth claims and their logic, but at least it helps to explain the strange-sounding suggestion that some of our beliefs — including perhaps our religious beliefs — may be groundless without being unreasonable.

1

Though he was captivated by philosophical questions and drawn toward philosophical doubts, Wittgenstein was never a skeptic. He never doubted that kind of ordinary truth which everyone takes for granted whenever not doing philosophy. To Wittgenstein the problems associated with skepticism, like other philosophical problems, presented themselves as high-grade confusions compounded partly out of insight but mostly

I
—
7

out of misunderstanding. Instead of answering the arguments of the skeptics, he treated their doubts as spurious and ill-founded, even though he was no more able than the skeptics themselves to furnish proofs for all his beliefs.

On the surface there was nothing particularly novel about this, since others, notably G. E. Moore, had responded to skepticism in much the same way.[3] Moore knew, of course, that our senses sometimes deceive us, that our memories often fail us, that science regularly unmasks the errors of common sense, and so on; but he could not see how such considerations could lead him to doubt those things of which he was absolutely certain. To take his famous example, Moore was certain that he had two hands; as he stood before a learned philosophical society exhibiting these two hands, *nothing* could make him doubt this fact. He did not bother to explain *how* he knew, but since he was sure that he *did* know, he did not think such an explanation was necessary. He was certain of his own certainty, so to speak, and for Moore that was enough to settle the matter: some things we know for sure and any philosophy which denies this fact is therefore in error.

Moore's argument, of course, did not really settle the skeptics' problem at all—at least not to the skeptics' satisfaction. Without explaining the reasons for his certainty, Moore failed to show that every possible doubt could be answered. Far from solving the problem, Moore's treatment actually exemplified the dilemma of skepticism in its purest form. On the one hand, the doubts of the skeptic *must* be groundless simply because we *are* certain about some things; on the other hand, so long as we cannot meet the doubts of the skeptic directly, our certainty seems gratuitous. Somewhere Moore's argument had gone wrong, leaving a loophole for the re-entry of the same old perplexities. The flaw in his argument, however, cannot be located simply by pointing out that he failed to secure his convictions against every conceivable doubt. Moore expected everyone to agree about such things as having hands, and he was right—we do agree in accepting a great number of such simple truisms as certainties. What Moore failed to show, however, is that being certain in this sense leaves no room for

I
8

philosophical doubts. After all, it is not enough to remind the skeptic that we are ordinarily certain about many things, since this is not something which he has forgotten. Rather, it has to be shown that the purely philosophical doubts which threaten such certainties on the level of abstract speculation are idle doubts, doubts which cannot and should not be taken seriously. It has to be shown, that is, that the purely speculative doubts of the skeptic do not even make sense. That is Wittgenstein's strategy.

Religious doubts, by contrast, *do* make sense, and we know how seriously we have to take them. Nonetheless, the religious believer who is confronted by the doubts and demands of the nonbeliever occupies a position analogous to that of the ordinary believer confronted by philosophical skepticism. Just as the ordinary believer finds himself at a loss for arguments in the face of philosophical skepticism, the religious believer usually finds himself unable to meet the critical demands of the nonbeliever. The nonbeliever usually wants *compelling* arguments, whereas the believer realizes that the beliefs at issue ultimately have to be accepted as articles of faith. Hence the believer usually does not take the lack of compelling arguments as seriously as the nonbeliever, not because the nonbeliever's doubts are idle, but because his demands cannot be answered in the way in which they are put. The religious believer, in other words, just like Moore, the ordinary believer, refuses to admit that his beliefs are arbitrary or unreasonable. They simply do not measure up to what the nonbeliever expects in the way of a rationally justified conviction.

We should not press this comparison too far too soon, however. The logic of religious belief is actually more complicated than the logic of Moore's commonsensical convictions, and it is best not to stress the similarities until we are in a position to explain the differences. The simpler case — Moore's case — comes first.

According to Wittgenstein, Moore went wrong in his treatment of the skeptics by presenting his certainties as things he *knew* to be true. By saying that he *knew* his assertions to be true, he invited the very question which he wanted to avoid:

how do we know? Had Moore maintained his certainty without representing his views as confirmed opinions, or had he simply brushed aside any doubts, Wittgenstein might not have objected; but for Moore to speak of knowing here misrepresented the logical status of his convictions. Whether or not one says that he *knows* such certainties to be true may seem a small matter, and it is — except when saying that one knows is meant to exclude the possibilities of doubt. That, however, was exactly what Moore was trying to do; namely, to bring out the fact that he was not and could not possibly be mistaken about such things as having hands. If he had been willing to admit the possibility of doubt about this, he might have been careful to say only that he *believed* that he had two hands, or that he *felt reasonably sure.* Yet that kind of truism is hardly a matter for conjecture; thus, it would have been even more misleading for him to use the kind of expression which would accommodate differences of opinion. To strengthen his statement, Moore claimed to *know — with certainty —* that he had two hands.

Unfortunately, the persuasive force of Moore's discussion outweighs its logic. From the skeptic's point of view, *any* knowledge claim requires a warrant; and as long as Moore cannot provide one, the possibility of a mistake will continue to provoke the skeptic's doubt. Of course, if Moore *does* know that he has two hands, then the *fact* that he has two hands follows with the inexorability with which "p" follows from "he knows 'p.' " Since the logical necessity of that inference ("p" from "he knows 'p' ") is easily confused with the necessity of "p" being true, Moore's argument (that he cannot possibly be mistaken) seems to succeed. Yet "p" is true only if "he knows 'p' " is true; and whether or not one knows something, as Wittgenstein reminds us, always takes some showing. In other words, if Moore does in fact know that he has two hands, then it must be true that he has these hands; and if it *must* be true, then he cannot possibly be mistaken. But does he know? That is the question.

The spectacle of Moore's certainty did establish one fact: Moore *felt certain* about having hands, etc. Yet this is a fact about Moore himself and does not guarantee the truth of his assertions. Even if Moore had never misplaced his confidence in those things he claimed to know for sure, this would still not mean that he could not possibly be mistaken. "One always forgets the expression 'I thought I knew' " (*OC* 12); which is to say, we are sometimes wrong about what we think we know, even when we *feel* certain. Of course, Moore wanted to claim more than a feeling of certainty; he *was* certain. He was not just surmising; he *knew*. If this is granted, then the rest of his argument follows. Yet the skeptic issues his challenge at just this point, demanding justification for *all* our knowledge claims, even those which seem most certain. Moore's unabashed claim that we know such things for sure simply begs the question.

In the question-begging character of Moore's argument, however, we see only a symptom of a more fundamental defect. The problem is not simply that Moore failed to show *how* he knew what he claimed to know; he played into the skeptic's hand by suggesting that his assertions were indeed verifiable. By saying that he knew that he had two hands, he implied that his having hands was a fact whose truth might be objectively established, as that is just what a knowledge claim is — a testable judgment. Furthermore, by saying that he knew *with certainty* that he had these two hands, he implied that a proper test would *demonstrate* the indubitability of his claim. Moore therefore made it seem as if his certainties were based on rational foundations of unimpeachable evidence, almost as if he were inviting the skeptic to ask for these hidden proofs. Moore himself never questioned the existence of such rational foundations, even though he was unable to produce them. He assumed that his knowledge *had* to have grounds, simply because he was *sure* of what he knew. He had to know *somehow*. There had to be grounds.[4]

What bothered Wittgenstein was the implication that evidential grounds are *perpetually* needed to justify reasonable convictions, at least for the philosopher if not for the everyday man. He saw, as Moore failed to see, that the possibility of doubt will never go away as long as rational grounds are needed to justify truth claims. He realized, that is, that the rational ideal of an objectively testable judgment is a two-edged sword. Wherever it applies it can cut both ways, requiring reasons to be given in support of a hypothesis but also allowing doubts to be urged against it. In effect, this carves out a permanent place for the logical possibility of doubt and gives the skeptic the right to demand logical grounds for belief. In many instances, of course, the evidence may leave us little or no room for doubting a well-established belief; but this means only that the doubts which have arisen so far have been answered, not that any further doubts are unthinkable or logically impossible. And as long as doubt is *logically* possible, the skeptic can press his case. Philosophical skepticism does not derive its force from any particular reasons for doubt; it draws its strength from the general possibility of error and the abstract possibility of finding new reasons for doubting old truths. How can we be absolutely sure of what we know as long as such possibilities exist? That is the problem.

Thus, the only way one can answer the skeptic is to show that doubt is sometimes completely out of place, that it does not even make sense to doubt some things, and that some things are certain not because our doubts have been answered but because these certainties leave speculative doubts without any logical foothold. If all our certainties are matters of knowledge, as Moore would have it, then possible doubts will find this foothold in the ever-present need for logical foundations. Knowledge claims presumably rest on justifiable grounds; if other knowledge claims serve to provide these grounds, then they *too* will require grounds, and so on. This never-ending need for further foundations keeps the skeptic going, and if one continually renews the right to demand rational grounds by offering more knowledge claims, the doubts of skeptics are bound to persist.

That is why Wittgenstein, though he admired Moore's dogged common sense, dismissed his treatment of philosophical skepticism in favor of a completely different strategy. Instead of trying to assure us that the indubitability of a cer-

I

12

tainty might be demonstrated by some yet-unknown anaylsis, Wittgenstein tried to show that we cannot always make sense of doubt, even when we cannot eliminate the purely abstract possibility of holding mistaken convictions. The doubts which the skeptic raises on this bare possibility carry no logical force, and when they carry no force, they require no answer. Once this becomes clear, one no longer feels responsible for answering every skeptical demand for justification, particularly when the beliefs in question are certainties of the kind Moore tried to defend. When that kind of truism is challenged, we find the possibility of an error simply unthinkable. We cannot answer the skeptic because we cannot understand his reasons for doubting such things, and we leave his questions unanswered because we find nothing substantial in their foundation. The skeptic takes this as a triumph, but Wittgenstein sided with the believer. Rather than defending a certainty on logical grounds, as if it were an insufficiently established hypothesis, Wittgenstein attacked the skeptic's right to demand that kind of justification.

To make his point, however, he had to overthrow one of the most entrenched assumptions of traditional philosophy. He had to show that the normal demand for rational justification cannot apply to every factual claim, and that the logical possibility of reasonable doubt diminishes as we approach the foundations of our judgments. In other words, he had to make it clear that all truth claims are not *hypotheses*, and that the beliefs which Moore wanted to defend as conclusively established hypotheses actually belong to another logical category altogether. Like Moore, he described the beliefs in this other category as "certainties." He occasionally lapsed into Moore's habit of referring to these beliefs as a type of knowledge, but only to indicate that certainties might be understood in a purely logical sense having nothing to do with psychological feelings of conviction. He wanted to distinguish such certainties, not only from psychological feelings of conviction, but also from the kind of confirmed belief which constitutes knowledge in a strict sense. Unlike Moore, therefore, he drew a distinction between knowledge and certainty, and he used this distinction to focus attention on a whole range of beliefs characterized by a remarkable logical feature—a peculiar immunity to doubt.

> 'Knowledge' and 'certainty' belong to different *categories*. They are not two 'mental states' like, say 'surmising' and 'being sure'; ... What interests us now is not being sure but knowledge. That is, we are interested in the fact that about certain empirical propositions no doubt can exist if making judgments is to be possible at all (*OC* 308).

Knowledge claims represent the *products* of our judgments, but our thinking involves various other beliefs as its *condition*—those beliefs "about which no doubt can exist if making judgments is to be possible at all." These are our certainties, the foundations for our thinking, and they cannot be surrendered in doubt without toppling entire systems of reasonable judgment. In this seemingly simple logical insight Wittgenstein found the solution to Moore's difficulties and disarmed the threat of philosophical skepticism.

Wittgenstein, of course, was not the first philosopher to realize that some facts have to be taken for granted if we are to form reasonable judgments about other factual claims. He was the first to flesh out this purely formal point with all of its substance. Few would argue that one proposition or another must serve as an assumed ground of judgment, but if we leave the point at this, it offers little help against the skeptic. Why assume this belief rather than another? Why not begin with another set of assumptions? As long as we have *options* here, such questions are bound to arise, bringing with them the same old skeptical doubts and demands. In fact, we do not have such open options. As Wittgenstein tried time and again to show, our understanding of reasonable judgments depends on a range of particular beliefs, so that we cannot maintain reasonable doubts and rational arguments while arbitrarily shifting our grounds. A reasonable person does not simply follow certain formal rules of inference in his thinking. He

I

14

grounds his judgments in particular assumptions which give substance to the notion of rational foundations and which make reasonable thinking a more concretely defined affair.

Wittgenstein never tried to list all these peculiarly indubitable certainties, since there are no definite boundaries to this class. He simply offered his own examples to go along with those of Moore.

> If anyone's arm is cut off, it will not
> grow back again (*OC* 274).
> The sun is not a hole in the vault of
> heaven (*OC* 104).
> Every living human being can be found to
> have bodily organs (*OC* 118).
> People have killed animals since earliest
> times and used the fur and bones for
> various purposes (*OC* 284).

How can these assertions be doubted? We tend to think that the truth of such propositions is questionable in principle, though odd in practice, because we can formulate the denials of these claims without producing self-contradictions. So we say that it is logically possible for such things to be false. Yet can we make any *sense* of these logical possibilities? Can we really think that the denials of these things might be true? The mere fact that we can formulate the denial of a proposition without contradicting ourselves does not provide any *reason* for doubt; it only shows that the proposition is not an "analytic" truth. Nor do we have a reason for doubting such a certainty if we can imagine some state of affairs in connection with its denial. We can picture a scene on an operating table where a person's skull is opened and found to contain sawdust; but this is a sheer fantasy of the imagination, and someone who was led by such a fanciful picture to think that we might have sawdust in our heads after all would rightly be taken for a fool.

Perhaps it is more plausible to imagine a case in which a man's arm after being cut off is made to grow back again. Yet if this is a more plausible case, it owes its plausibility to the fact that we can fill out this picture with various pertinent facts; e.g., that medical science is pressing forward with new discoveries in genetics, the mechanisms of regeneration are being discovered in other life forms, and so on. The more such facts as these can be taken into account, the more likely it seems that the regeneration of a limb might be possible. If we now question the commonsense truism that a severed limb will not grow back, though, the ground of our doubt is not the picture conjured up in imagination, but the facts that we bring to the picture. Without such facts, grounds for doubt are simply lacking, and the "possibility" that we might be wrong about these things remains an empty notion.

In short, doubt, too, requires a ground; otherwise it never acquires the force of a reasonable suspicion. To doubt something for no reason at all is to think idly, and idle doubts do not have to be answered. In fact, idle doubts *cannot* be answered unless one knows what lies behind them. The reason for this is that we must know how to weigh reasons for belief against reasons for doubt if we are to make reasonable judgments, but without a reason for doubt, we do not know what kind of opposing judgment is called for. *Groundless* doubts exert no leverage in our thinking because they do not fit into the determination of truth and falsity in any definite way. Because they presume no particular foundation for judgment, they call for no particular response. We do not even know what to *count* as a reasonable reply to such doubts. Only a *reason* can sharpen the edge of a doubt, so that it cuts against a belief and demands a response.

The remarkable thing about the propositions which Moore claimed to know is that, while we have no logically prior grounds for affirming them, we have no grounds for doubting them either. One might like to say a good deal in connection with such certainties in the face of professed doubts, and the things one says here might be described as "reasons"; but it would not be clear that these "reasons" had any weight in settling the issue at hand.

If someone said to me that he doubted whether he had a body I should take him to be a half-wit. But I

I
___
16

shouldn't know what it would mean to try to convince him that he had one. And if I said something,
and that had removed his doubt, I should not know
how or why (*OC* 257).

If someone could doubt that he has a body, then he could
presumably doubt any of the myriad of facts (e.g., that he has a
mouth with which he expresses these doubts) which one would
like to mention in opposition to his doubt. Such a doubt infects
virtually everything that we ordinarily take for granted, leaving us at a loss for something to count on as a secure foundation of judgment. Here nothing seems any more certain than
the belief in question, and therefore nothing seems to provide
the firmer ground that an *argument* would require.

What then could serve the doubter as a reason for doubt?
What could the skeptic know which is any more certain than
having a body? And what could give him a reason for thinking
otherwise? Without some foundation of reliable truths, one
who doubts something cannot ground his own suspicions in
fact; and when those truths which ordinarily furnish this kind
of foundation are themselves in doubt, we no longer know what
truths, if any, can be trusted as the basis for a reasonable
response. Nothing can be settled where everything is in doubt.
In such a case, everything does not collapse in doubt, as the
skeptic would have it; the force of the skeptic's doubt simply
becomes unintelligible.

This example of someone who doubts that he has a body is
but one of many that Wittgenstein puts before us to show that
the peculiar doubts of the skeptic are not only odd in practice
but *logically* out of place. In learning how to make critical
judgments, one learns to rely on an indefinite number of
unquestioned truths; these truths form what Wittgenstein
called "the inherited background against which I distinguish
true and false" (*OC* 162). They make up our "world picture" (*OC*
162), or our "frame of reference" (*OC* 83). None of these descriptions is particularly important apart from the single point
of interest—"the fact that about certain empirical propositions
no doubt can exist if making judgments is to be possible at all."

To put it more generally, there is a difference in logical status of various claims to fact. Since the truth of some is required as a condition for the possibility of judging others, some occupy a kind of axiomatic status. These truths are certain not because their truth can be derived from propositions that are still more certain, but because the way in which we adjudicate other truth claims anchors them too deeply for doubt in our thinking. Unlike hypotheses, which can stand to be confirmed or disconfirmed *in the course of our judgments,* these certainties "lie apart from the route traveled by inquiry." Idle doubts cannot touch them.

Ironically, the propositions which Moore claimed to *know,* as if he had confirmed them as hypotheses, represent just such axiom-like beliefs. One cannot seriously entertain doubts about these things without unhinging empirical inquiry altogether. For if one cannot be sure that he has a body, or hands, or that he has been living on or very close to the surface of the earth, then he cannot be sure of anything. Mere observation can no longer provide any evidence, and empirical arguments cannot find a place to begin. All ordinary evidence wilts under suspicion. Yet no one needs to doubt such things, since the skeptic has no way of substantiating his doubts without returning to the same assumptions of rational thinking. Moore, therefore, did not have to defend his certainty by staking out any knowledge claims. His certainty was not the product of prior judgments and should not have been expressed as if it were. Consequently, he made his first mistake as soon as he said, "I know . . ."

> One says 'I know' when one is ready to give compelling grounds. 'I know' relates to a possibility of demonstrating the truth. Whether one knows or not can come to light, assuming that he is convinced of it.
>
> But if what he believes is of such a kind that the grounds that he can give are no surer than his assertion, then he cannot say that he knows what he believes (*OC* 243).

No grounds that Moore might have given could be any more certain than his own commonsense convictions, so instead of allowing for the possibility of a reasonable argument here, he should have turned his efforts toward exposing the unreasonableness of the skeptic's demand. Where there are grounds for adjudication, there is always the possibility that doubt might gain a foothold; but where groundless doubts are aimed at the foundation of our judgments, they undermine the only means we have for taking them seriously. If Moore had seen this point, he might have anticipated Wittgenstein in dismissing the purely speculative doubts of the philosophical skeptic with a clearer conscience. The logic of reasonable judgment gives us all that right.

2

Whether or not it gives us the right to dismiss *religious* doubts, however, is another question. Such doubts are certainly not idle; that we can say for sure. Yet in the face of these doubts we may be too quick to defend religious beliefs as Moore defended his certainties, i.e., as hypotheses. Moore's certainties are not the only beliefs that differ from knowledge claims; religious assertions do not fit that description either. Perhaps religious claims can no more be *grounded* than certainties, and perhaps their lack of grounds should not be held against them. Wittgenstein evidently thought so, for in his few remarks on the subject he refused to treat religious beliefs as testable hypotheses. Yet one should not press Wittgenstein's remarks into the service of theology without introducing some qualifications.

For one thing, today's certainties may be tomorrow's mistakes, and Wittgenstein himself unwittingly provides an example.

Suppose some adult had told a child that he had been on the moon. The child tells me the story, and I say it was only a joke, the man hadn't been on the moon; the moon is a long way off and it is impossible to climb up there or fly there.—If now the child insists, saying perhaps there is a way of getting there which I don't know, etc. what reply could I make to him? (*OC* 106).

Now, of course, we know that men have been to the moon, and the idea of "flying to the moon" is no longer so unthinkable. What was once a certainty—that no one has ever been to the moon—is now not only dubious but known to be false.

Those who smile at this, as if it showed how easily a philosopher can be misled by the assumptions of his day, are missing the point. Wittgenstein never argued that all those things which we now take for granted will always be certain, but that certainties will not become any less certain without specific reasons for doubt.

'I *know* that I have never been on the moon.' That sounds quite different in the circumstances which actually hold [c. 1950], to the way it would sound if a good many men had been on the moon, and some perhaps without knowing it. In *this* case one could give grounds for this knowledge (*OC* 111).

Today the circumstances which Wittgenstein once imagined do hold. We know how it is possible to get to the moon; thus we know what it would mean to give reasons for or against the claim that someone, say a particular Russian cosmonaut, had actually been there. The point is not that our certainties are timeless, then, but that those beliefs which lie at the foundation of our judgments cannot be doubted in any but an idle way *until* they can be reassessed as hypotheses. The mere fact that this has happened to some certainties in the past does not give us grounds for doubting others, for our past mistakes do not focus suspicion anywhere in particular among our present beliefs. Does the fact that men have been on the moon make it any less certain that the world is older than any living human being or that George Washington had to breathe during his term of office? Perhaps there are some things which are less certain now—e.g., that no one can burrow down to the center of the earth—but if this has something to do with the one-time certainty that no one can fly to the moon, it has to do with the technological developments which made space travel possible (e.g., heat-resistant metals) and not with the general fact that we have sometimes had to revoke some of our certainties. So the distinction between certainties and hypotheses still stands, even if particular propositions shift from time to time from one category into the other.

The distinction also stands in spite of the fact that we cannot assign some propositions clearly to one category or the other. The certainty of a historical claim, for example, varies from the absolute certainty that the world has a past to the highly dubious conjecture that Hitler is alive and well in Argentina. Between these two extremes we find a continuous gradation of more or less reliable facts, many of which we could not definitely identify as certainties. Yet this does not mean that the distinction between certainties and hypotheses should be abandoned, since the fact remains that some historical claims must provide the framework in which we settle our doubts about others.

More interesting and more troubling is the fact that the same proposition can sometimes be certain and sometimes be dubious. With some certainties it takes nothing more than a change of context to furnish a reason for doubt. If after an accident, for example, one wakes up in the hospital with his limbs completely bandaged, he might well wonder if he still has two hands. But this is plainly an unusual circumstance, and *normally* one does not have to look, or to feel, to arrive at a conclusion about the existence of one's own hands. To clarify the logical status of a certainty, then, one would like to be able to specify the normal circumstances which keep our doubts at bay. The trouble is that this cannot be done. Even if we could come up with a "rule of normal circumstances," we would still have to rely on its application to identify exceptions. One might say, "Whenever you can *see* something, you need not doubt its existence"; but we know that there are abnormal circumstances in which this rule does not hold. So one might say, "Whenever you see something in adequate light with unimpaired vision, you needn't doubt its existence." Yet here too there are exceptions, and such exceptions will plague any such rule, unless one insures the rule gratuitously by adding a "normal circumstance" clause. The conditions for understanding what is "normal" and the conditions for understanding when to doubt and when not to doubt *are the same.* In either case one must see reasonable judgment *illustrated* by regular practice.

Moreover, since making judgments is always related to some encompassing activity, it is ultimately our common practice which holds our certainties in place. We treat some things as unquestionably reliable facts and subject other claims to tests, and our procedure here *illustrates* rational judgment. It shows what a reasonable person accepts without question as he subjects other beliefs to critical examination. If this sounds strange, it is because we usually regard our practice as a *consequence* of reasonable judgment, not as a determining factor in it. Most of the time an agreement in practice does not produce an agreement in belief, but the other way around—an agreement in belief leads to an agreement in practice. Yet this commonsensical observation applies only to those cases in which it is possible to test a belief before acting on it, and this is not always possible. When faced with those beliefs which serve as prior conditions for our judgments, we lack the logical means of establishing their truth or falsity on more certain grounds. Then affirming a belief and acting on it become virtually indistinguishable. In fact, we usually don't affirm the kind of certainties Wittgenstein had in mind in any *explicit* way at all. In our judgments of other matters we simply act without doubt about such things. We do not even bother to formulate them as assertions; neither do we expect anyone else to—so long as he is a reasonable person who has learned, as we have, what it means to think in a responsible and critical way.

The way in which a historian assembles evidence, for example—the way in which he implicitly assumes certain dates as points of reference and the way in which he relies on certain facts as he focuses his critical questions—all this shows a complete absence of doubt about a myriad of unstated historical beliefs. Thus one who sets out to clarify say, the causes and circumstances of Captain Cook's death in the Pacific Islands, approaches the problem without any doubt about the fact that Cook was engaged in a voyage of exploration, or that he had a number of sailors under his command. Still less does one doubt that Cook and his men had to eat to stay alive, that the extant records of the event were written by human beings, or that there was such a place as England in those days. Perhaps we would be willing to doubt that Cook ever visited the Pacific if some shred of evidence could be found to oppose everything which says that he did, but we cannot conceive how something like the existence of England in the eighteenth century could be doubted. That is something which we have learned to accept in learning how to pursue historical explanations in the first place; and thus the framework of critical historical thinking leaves this certainty completely untouched by doubt. To doubt it would leave us too disoriented to know how to go on with historical inquiry. The essential agreement of practice which enables us to settle historical questions by consulting the facts would utterly dissolve. It would dissolve, that is, if we took such doubts seriously; but of course we do not, and the reason we do not is that we do not have to. Once we know how to think in critical historical terms, our judgments proceed apace on the foundations provided by our certainties, and that is reason enough for our trust.

If someone *did* doubt such a thing as the existence of England in the past, we would suppose that he was joking, or that he was a half-wit, or that he was too confused to know what he was saying—unless the one who professed such doubts was a child, in which case we would respond with *instruction*, not argument. In giving the child this instruction, we would give assurances that the existence of England is something to rely on—indeed, that it is a fact that *must* be relied on in making further inquiries. A reasonable person (i.e., one who has learned to reason historically) just does not question such a thing. So in teaching a person how to make reasonable judgments, we teach not only *methods* but *facts*—and accepting these facts is part of the method. Later perhaps we may discover some reasons to question one or another of these facts; but the manner of our thinking will still retain its tie to many of those beliefs which make up its matter.

Perhaps this connection between our understanding of rational methods of judgment and our judgments themselves will be easier to understand if we put the point in terms of *concepts* and beliefs associated with them. We tell a child all sorts of things about England in order to teach him what the word "England" means; and as a result, the child's concept of England becomes bound up with various bits of information. Some of this information may turn out to be false without affecting one's understanding of the concept — but not all of it. If England never had kings, never fought wars with other nations, and never had its shores washed by the North Sea, we would no longer know what "England" meant. Much the same connection between facts and concepts holds elsewhere. If Aristotle never wrote philosophy books, never met Plato, never lived in Greece, etc., then we would not know who Aristotle was. If human beings did not have bodily organs, did not have to eat to stay alive, did not die, and so on, then our understanding of what a human being is would fall apart. So even to agree in the language we use, to share a common understanding of concepts, we must set some beliefs aside from reasonable doubt.

Seeing that an understanding of concepts usually presumes some unquestioned acceptance of certain facts represents a remarkable logical insight. It forces us to loosen some of the traditional categories of logical analysis, such as the distinction between definitions and factual assertions, or between analytic truths and synthetic judgments. Wittgenstein's certainties resemble definitions in certain respects, yet they are not true *by definition.* At least their truth is not a matter of conventional stipulation; for if England did have kings or Aristotle did write philosophy books, it is not because we decided to think that way. Those empirical beliefs which occupy the axiomatic role of certainties, then, are not *analytic* in the technical sense. Their denials are not always self-contradictions. Yet to make room for the logical possibility

I

that these certainties might be false, we have to imagine such extraordinary circumstances that this possibility dwindles to the idlest speculation. On the other hand, calling these certainties "synthetic" fails to shed any light on their peculiar logical status as grounds and conditions for reasonable thinking. They seem much closer to Kant's "synthetic a priori" truths; yet that is not quite right either. No hard and fast line divides the class of certainties from the class of knowledge claims (or hypotheses), and the status of individual beliefs sometimes changes. Unlike metaphysical absolutes, then, our empirical certainties cannot be "transcendentally deduced" as necessary assumptions of all rational thought. They have only the "necessity" of working assumptions in our *own* rational practice. Nothing absolute stands behind them, only the particular ways in which we have come to understand and assess the world around us.

Still, I do not mean to suggest that the grounds of certainty upon which we conduct our empirical inquiries or daily discourses are arbitrary. Neither did Wittgenstein. Perhaps he should have said more to prevent misunderstanding on this point, but he was too anxious to avoid the mistake that Moore and the skeptics had both made in approaching every belief as an adjudicable hypothesis. The point he wanted to make, and the one we are to keep in mind, is that the logical possibility of justification varies according to the logical status of the beliefs in question. The ideal of confirming every belief as a well-grounded hypothesis ceases to apply as we reach the bedrock of our thinking. Perhaps some other type of rationale applies instead; but having brought us this far, Wittgenstein leaves us with nothing more to go on. If there is any further question of justification here, it is not one of discovering deeper strata of incorrigible certainties (as Moore thought), but one of defending our axiomatic convictions *in the absence of any further foundations.*

In any case, some beliefs are so deeply entrenched in our thinking that it makes no sense to treat them as debatable hypotheses. They cannot be measured against any more certain judgments of fact, and their credibility is not a function of independent evidence. They permit no justification on prior logical grounds, but neither do they require it. The logic of reasonable judgments exempts them from doubt.

3

The credibility of religious beliefs may not be a function of evidence either. Yet they are obviously not exempt from doubt, and so they hardly qualify as *certainties.* Only in primitive and homogeneous societies, where religious concepts are thoroughly integrated into everyday thought and practice, could religious beliefs play the kind of pivotal role which would immunize them against doubt. In such societies, if any exist, religious beliefs would have to be inseparable from other systems of judgment, so that the primitive skeptic would have nothing to fall back on as an alternative means of framing his descriptions and accounts of experience. The whole fabric of his beliefs would have to be such that the loosening of the religious ones (or those that look religious to us) would unravel the whole cloth. In cases like this we might describe the axiomatic beliefs of the participants as "certainties" in a sense, and this might even be illuminating. Instead of encouraging us to speculate about some hidden chain of reasoning lying behind primitive religious beliefs, such as the belief in *mana* or totems, it would redirect our attention to the surrounding patterns of thinking which hold these beliefs in place and which leave the believer nowhere else to stand as a basis for doubt.[5] Yet even if we *did* describe these underlying beliefs as "certainties," this would only mean that they play a foundational role in the thinking of the participants—i.e., that they represent certainties *for them.* For us, who have learned to frame our inquiries in quite different and more varied ways, such "certainties" are not only dubious but virtually unthinkable.

This last point is important. The fact that one can doubt a certainty from the "outside," so to speak, shows that Wittgenstein overstated his case against groundless doubts. He repeatedly said that doubt requires a ground, as if we could not doubt an assertion in any significant way unless we had some specific reason for doubt (*OC* 122, 323, 372, 458). In context, one can see why he said this; but as a generalization about the nature of doubt, the claim will not stand up. We can doubt *alien* propositions for no other reason than that we simply do not know what to make of them. We need not have any counter-evidence to weigh against favorable evidence for belief; we simply might not know how to assimilate a belief to any conceivable pattern of reasonable judgment. When that happens, the implausibility of a belief does not arise from its poor standing in the light of the evidence which we bring to it. It comes from the fact that we are unable to give it *any* logical standing in our thinking—either as a hypothesis or as a foundational belief. And that is all that it takes to make it dubious.

To doubt a remote belief from a primitive society, then, we do not have to treat it as a hypothesis to be torn down on evidential grounds. We can acknowledge the axiom-like role which the belief plays in the thinking of others without giving it any role whatsoever in our own. Having no idea what the point of such a belief may be, and being unable to fit it into any of our own ways of thinking, we may not know what it would mean to affirm the belief itself *or* its denial. And until we know that, we can refuse to consider it even as a candidate for rational adjudication. For this kind of doubt we need no special excuse; the completely alien character of various primitive beliefs gives us reason enough for being suspicious.

Thus, there is a crucial difference between doubting the certainties of others and doubting our own. Doubting the former leaves everything we know as good judgment intact, while doubting the latter undermines the very grounds on which we stand. In the case of our own certainties, we have no alternative foundations to rely on; but in the case of culturally alien beliefs, we *do* have an alternative—namely, everything that we already know as critical thinking and good judgment. Skepticism here does not unhinge our normal reasonings; it reflects a natural reaction to the abnormal and unassimilable. Since nothing holds such alien beliefs in place *for us*, the burden of answering our doubts falls on the side of the believer.

The same holds true when the beliefs in question are familiar Judeo-Christian beliefs. Since we have secular alternatives to theistic ways of thinking, we do not depend on the belief in God so thoroughly that all our reasonings would collapse without it. Even those who have grown up believing in God can lose their faith without losing their ability to think about the world in a myriad of other ways. After all, there are many people who share our general education and our sense of good judgment but who do not share our religious views. Thus we know that our religious beliefs, whatever they may be, constitute a kind of overlay in our thinking, an overlay which could be removed without undermining all our conceptual capacities. Those who *do* lose their religious beliefs may be troubled by the loss of the particular perspective which these beliefs provided; but they can still *think* about their religious concerns. They can still make some judgments about themselves, their happiness, their life prospects, and so on. Religious doubts, therefore, even if they are groundless, do not destroy themselves in the manner of idle speculative doubts. Nor can religious skepticism be turned aside in the same way that philosophical skepticism can be dismissed. One simply does not *need* any particular reason for not being religious. No counter-evidence against the existence of God or the authority of scripture is required to justify religious doubts. It is enough simply to have learned to think and live without such beliefs.

Seeing that a religious skeptic has a right to his doubts, believers can be expected to worry about a response. As this anxiety mounts, the tendency which overcame Moore in his defense of commonsense convictions—the tendency to treat every belief as if it were a hypothesis—becomes almost irresistible. The skeptic deserves an answer to his doubts, and the only way to provide it seems to be in the form of objective evidence. Without such evidence, the groundlessness of religious assertions makes them seem arbitrary and unwarranted. What else are we to think? Doubt, it seems, would not be a serious matter unless there was some danger of being mistaken in matters of faith; and if nothing can be done to minimize this danger, it is hard to see how any ungrounded religious beliefs could be reasonably held. Some kind of evidence must apply. Otherwise, the whole business can have little to do with reason, or with truth.

Even so, compelling evidence is no more to be expected for religious beliefs than it is for certainties; and the reason is the same in both cases. Like certainties, from which they differ in almost every other respect, religious beliefs play a governing role in the thinking of believers. They ground the believer's characteristic judgments and fix his religious concepts, so that his outlook assumes its peculiarly religious quality through his reliance on these pivotal beliefs. This does not mean that one can take the truth of religious beliefs, like the truth of certainties, for granted; but it does mean that religious beliefs and certainties have a comparable relation to *practice.* The believer's practice in conforming to his beliefs is not derived from a prior judgment about their truth; his affirmation of basic religious beliefs *coincides* with the entry into some new pattern of agreement in the way he thinks. To break this internal connection between affirming religious beliefs and entering into new ways of thinking, as if one could judge a religious belief as an hypothesis *before* acting on it, would skew the significance which these beliefs bear as regulative ideas. It would rob religious teachings of their foundational roles in instituting new *types* of judgment, so that the issues at stake would lose much of their meaning. One could then "believe" in religious claims without submitting one's concerns to any new form of understanding.

Thus—and this is the important point—the notorious difficulty of justifying religious assertions on evidential grounds actually reflects their logical role. We usually assume that the dubiousness of religious claims comes from lack of evidence, but the adoption of a religious view of life requires more than evidence. It requires a change in the way of thinking, the practice, which underlies the interpretation and use of evidence. Instead of requiring more in the way of familiar rational grounds, faith claims represent new grounds for a new species of judgment. When these new grounds are proposed, the evidence which serves the nonbeliever as a basis of judgment becomes a part of the issue and ceases to offer any means toward its resolution.

In *On Certainty,* Wittgenstein said very little about religious beliefs; but when he did talk about them, that was the point he wanted to make. He objected to the idea that religious beliefs represent *mistakes* of some kind, as if nonbelievers had the proper grounds to identify such mistakes. He did not want to say that religious beliefs were discernibly true, either. He simply wanted to distinguish religious disagreements from the kind of issue in which true and false judgments can be sorted out on common grounds. One who does not think that a religious belief is true need not assume that the belief rests on weak evidence or a faulty chain of inference. That is the wrong way to put it.

Catholics, to take one of Wittgenstein's examples, believe "that in certain circumstances a wafer completely changes in nature," while "all evidence proves the contrary" (*OC* 239). Can it be that Catholics base their belief on the visual evidence – or on anything else which nonbelievers understand as evidence? No, the believer does not treat his belief as a matter of evidence to begin with, and so one cannot say that he is making that kind of wild inference. Similarly, certain *"very* intelligent and well-educated people believe in the story of creation in the Bible, while others hold it as proven false, and the grounds of the latter are well known to the former" (*OC* 336). Wittgenstein emphasizes the intelligence and education of such believers to remind us that there are people who know very well how to think scientifically but who plainly do not regard the creation story as something to be upheld by science. To construe the facts of geological science as evidence for the biblical account is so far-fetched that we can discount the possibility that educated believers have taken this evidence and simply, as it were, *miscalculated.* Rather, they do their sums according to a wholly different system of thinking.

Believers and nonbelievers stand so far apart on such matters that they lack the common ground needed to resolve their differences. The believer acknowledges the nonbeliever's evidence without giving it any weight; while the nonbeliever, because he does not know what else to use as evidence, dismisses the believer's claims as completely groundless and irrational. So the disagreement here extends beyond an objectively resolvable dispute; it reaches down into the framework where reasons for belief and reasons for doubt are defined. Telling appeals to the facts are no longer possible, because the disputants differ in what they count as a relevant appeal. Yet if the creation story were a geological hypothesis, no such complications would exist. Indeed, if it were any kind of hypothesis, then it would be logically possible to ground one's judgment in the relevant evidence and then this evidence—"the facts"—would count. As it is, though, religious claims resist any decisive adjudication according to factual evidence, and believers and nonbelievers remain at cross-purposes in their disputes.

From this point of view, one can see why one might describe religious beliefs as "articles of faith." Such beliefs are not proposals to be tested on familiar grounds; they are proposals for erecting new ways of thinking on new grounds. That makes them comparable to certainties in terms of the patterns of thinking and living which surround them; but it does not protect them from doubt. One who would be religious still needs reasons of *some* kind to disarm his doubts.

4

At this point, however, Wittgenstein's clues dwindle to almost nothing. Only the logical oddity of religious assertions seems clear. They resemble certainties without being certain, they play axiomatic roles without being unquestionably reliable, and they waver before doubt without any particular reasons being urged against them. Perhaps they are *potentially* certain—candidates, so to speak, for the logical role of a certainty. In view of so many secular alternatives, however, it is hard to see how any religious belief could bear enough weight in our thinking to make it indispensable. Such beliefs are much too optional and variable to be immunized against doubt in that way. Whatever else they may be, therefore, they cannot be certainties.

We seem to be left, then, with the following choice: either we return to the idea that religious assertions are to be judged as hypotheses, or we give up the assumption that they are *bona fide* claims to truth. Neither alternative is very satisfying: the first leads directly to the unsolved problem of how religious claims about transcendent realities might conceivably be verified, and the second fails to account for the seriousness of doubt and the need for assurances in questions of faith. This dilemma, however, is a false one. Religious beliefs, despite all their peculiarities — their resistance to verification, their regulative roles, and their vulnerability to groundless doubts — are not unique. They share these logical features with a class of beliefs which are neither hypotheses nor common-place truisms. We call this wider class of beliefs "principles," or in some cases "fundamental principles," and we include many of these principles among the most reasonable of all our beliefs. Like certainties, they play a logical role which makes it virtually impossible to treat them as hypotheses — impossible, that is, without upsetting a whole domain of thought which is conditioned by them. And like certainties, the practice which surrounds them holds them in place as axiomatic premises of good judgment. Yet they are not so widely shared or universally understood that their truth can be taken for granted. Their truth is more like that of religious beliefs — a matter of faith.

Certainties, in other words, are not the only "groundless" beliefs which appropriately figure into our discourse. Certainties settle into the groundwork of our reasoning at rudimentary levels, where conventional ideas of reasonable procedure leave little room for intelligible disagreement. Principles govern higher levels of judgment in which our conventions are not so widely shared or solidly established. Thus, when principles are at issue, all that we know is that our experience calls for some form of further explanation or interpretation, something beyond a rudimentary description. To frame these higher orders of inquiry we lay down some definitive postulates as governing principles, hoping that the judgments to be made in accordance with these principles will yield the understanding which we seek. That is why principles, whether they are moral or scientific, aesthetic or economic, all have to be *mastered.* Their adoption requires new discipline in one's thinking, so that a new form of understanding might be achieved.

The same can be said of religious beliefs. In fact, we speak of religious "principles" just as easily as we do of any other kind; and all of the general characteristics of principles seem to fit. To believe in religious principles one has to abide by them; to appreciate them one has to master them; but to doubt them one has only to stand outside them, unwilling or unable to enter the domain in which they promise their peculiar form of understanding.

The only trouble with this comparison is that the logical features of principles are not much clearer than those of religious beliefs. Wittgenstein drew no finer distinctions between principles and certainties, or between one kind of certainty and another; nor has any other philosopher tried to sort out the variety of beliefs which can be reasonably held without being grounded. So before the comparison of matters of faith with matters of principle can be very illuminating, the crucial questions one would like to ask about the nature of principles, about their cognitive value and the possibility of their justification, have to be answered. So far the idea that religious claims function as principles, as groundless beliefs of a higher order than certainties, is only a promising suggestion.

I

NOTES

1. Ludwig Wittgenstein, *On Certainty* (New York: J. J. Harper, 1969); hereafter referred to in the text as *OC* followed by Wittgenstein's entry numbers.

2. Ludwig Wittgenstein, *Lectures and Conversations on Aesthetics, Psychology and Religious Belief*, ed. Cyril Barrett (Berkeley: University of California Press, 1967).

3. G. E. Moore, "Proof of an External World," in his *Philosophical Papers* (New York: MacMillan, 1949), pp. 126-48. See also his "A Defense of Common Sense," pp. 32-59.

4. Apparently he thought that his certainties could be broken down into simpler observational truths, so that the reconstruction of this analysis would demonstrate the logical grounds of his certitude. See "A Defense of Common Sense," *Philosophical Papers*, pp. 37f.

5. Notice that it is not the *social* patterns which hold such "certainties" in place; it is the pattern of *thinking* which requires reasonable doubts to be raised on the same familiar grounds which these certainties themselves provide. Presumably, the ways in which social structures reinforce beliefs do not prevent the *logical* possibilities of doubt, either for the observers of a primitive society or for its participants.

II
MATTERS OF FAITH AND
MATTERS OF PRINCIPLE

Principles used to be the stock in trade of philosophers. Their most important and controversial ideas were always advanced as principles of one kind or another. Yet philosophers do not often speak of principles any more.[1] Apparently the term carries too many associations with speculative philosophy to suit the mood of analysis or to survive in its technical vocabulary. Nevertheless, it is the business of analytic philosophy to refine such terms, so that our intellectual difficulties — in this case, questions of principle — can be rid of confusion and seen more clearly for what they are. Few other terms, in fact, would make better candidates for careful analysis.

To see how important the concept of a principle is, one need only think of the range of issues which we describe as matters of principle. Typically, these issues concern not just one item of dispute but alternative approaches to a whole range of issues — to moral questions, political disputes, psychological diagnoses, and so on. Religious disputes are simply one more example of the same kind, for they reflect the kind of disagreement in which people do not see eye to eye in their thinking because their governing beliefs conflict. With no clear understanding of the logic of principles, though, we are apt to let this insight pass with the admission that there is something right about it — instead of seeing that the use of the term "principle" here is *exactly* right. Matters of faith *are* matters of principle. It is just not clear what this means about the reasonableness of faith without a better account of principles in general.

1

We all have at least a vague idea of what principles are. They are beliefs of a peculiarly *basic* sort; they play a formative role in our judgments, yet they are not derived from any prior judgments. Thus, if pressed to a definition, one could say that principles are indemonstrable assertions that sustain and regulate further judgment. This definition may not cover every use of the term "principle" in common speech — some "principles" are not assertions at all, for example; they are simply general *rules*. Yet it points us in the direction in which we must go if we are to refine the concept, to sort out its ambiguities, and to apply it to religious beliefs. In effect, it simply reaffirms our sense that there are some beliefs which are qualitatively more fundamental than others, which play a normative role in our thinking, and which therefore belong in a class by themselves. The difficulty, of course, is to make all this clear.

Just what does it mean, for example, for a principle to be "fundamental"? When we speak of "first principles," we usually mean that they are "first" or "fundamental" in the sense that they cannot be derived from any more general or more reliable premises. Such principles occupy a logical status akin to that of axioms in a formal system; we do not establish them on prior grounds, we *use* them as grounds. Yet most systems of belief in which we rely on fundamental principles are not formal, axiomatized systems; and the indemonstrable character of these principles is not simply a matter of their being underived. Many more plebian assumptions — Wittgenstein's "certainties" — are also underived, since their truth is generally as certain as anything which could be offered in their support. Yet this is not the case with principles. Their relation to logical grounds is more complicated than that.

To bring out the type-difference between certainties and principles, we need to distinguish them both from a sharper conception of hypotheses. Hypotheses are testable asser- tions — testable in the general sense of being subject to one or another form of objective adjudication. Their "agreement with reality," as one could say, is subject to determination "by the facts," not by personal preference or by common convention. Or, to put the same point in another way, the question of their truth or falsity can be independently approached by way of the grounds needed for their support (which is why hypotheses need to be well-grounded to be reasonable). This, to be sure, is not the only sense in which the term "hypothesis" is used. In a narrower sense of the word hypotheses are testable generali- zations designed to develop *theories*, but the role of hypothe- ses in generating predictions and in testing theories obviously depends on the possibility of their own testing "by the facts." So the meaning of the term can easily be expanded to include *any* assertion which is subject to adjudication on independent grounds.

This definition can be stated in more technical language by saying that hypotheses must have independently specifiable truth conditions. The truth conditions of a proposition are simply those things which must be the case if it is true, and in this trivial sense every meaningful proposition has truth condi- tions. We can always assign truth conditions to a proposition "p" by saying that *p* must be the case if it is true. In some cases, however, an assertion does not have to be repeated in this way to say what its truth or falsity depends on. Instead, one can explain what must be the case if "p" is true in terms of an equivalent set of propositions, "a,b,c . . . n." These other pro- positions represent *entailments* of "p"; and as long as this list of entailments does not include "p" itself, or any other proposi- tion so closely related to "p" that its truth cannot be told without prior knowledge of "p's" truth, then "p's" truth condi- tions can be said to be *independently specifiable*. And its truth or falsity can be said to depend on these independent matters of fact.

To take a simple example, if we say something like "Arthur has tuberculosis," we can reformulate this hypothesis in terms of other questions about Arthur — e.g., have tubercles begun to form in his body, is a certain bacillus present, etc. Since we can address these other questions without already knowing that Arthur has the disease, we can use them to *test* the claim that he does. As long as having tuberculosis entails having a certain bacillus and entails having tubercles, the presence or absence of these conditions will confirm or disconfirm the diagnosis. This, admittedly, is a rather simple and somewhat artificial picture of the confirmation and disconfirmation of hypotheses, but it does illustrate a crucial feature of their logic. The claim that Arthur has tuberculosis qualifies as a hypothesis, not because we can in fact carry out a test of its truth but because the question of its truth or falsity can be reformulated in terms of other matters of fact — and this makes its measurement "by the facts" *logically* possible. The same holds true of all hypotheses: whenever a proposition's entailments can be independently articulated and separately judged, that proposition can be described as a hypothesis.[2]

It is easy to see that this is not an arbitrary definition. As long as we use the term "hypothesis" to include every truth claim whose agreement with reality can be tested according to fact, then being a hypothesis, being objectively adjudicable, and having independent truth conditions all come to the same thing. One checks a hypothesis against the facts simply by seeing if its truth conditions are fulfilled. We do not compare it with "reality in itself," so to speak. We invoke "reality" in the form of other true propositions, so that we actually compare a hypothesis with reality by seeing if these other propositions represent the fulfillment of its truth conditions. If the facts match its entailments, the hypothesis is corroborated; if the facts contradict one or more of its entailments, it is falsified. The important thing about all this is that we have some *independent* means of judgment, supplied by the independence of an assertion's truth conditions. For as long as we can separate our judgments of a proposition's entailments from a judgment of the proposition itself, we can *rest* the question of its truth or falsity on these other determinants. If we could not do this, objective judgment by independent criteria would not be possible. We could not leave the matter for the facts to decide.

This point about objective testing is worth emphasizing because independent testability is a very distinctive logical feature: some kinds of assertions have it, others do not. Hypotheses all have it, principles generally lack it. Certainties, oddly enough, sometimes have it and sometimes do not. Indeed, this is the point where finer distinctions between all these beliefs need to be drawn. Neither certainties nor principles, for example, lack entailments and truth conditions altogether; it is just that the entailments which they do have do not enable their truth or falsity to be told. The reasons for this vary, and it is vitally important to see why. Not every "groundless" belief shares the same logic.

To see what I mean, let us take the case of certainties first. All of the beliefs which Wittgenstein described as certainties were, in ordinary circumstances, more reasonable to believe than to doubt. Beyond that they showed little homogeneity.[3] Some of them, in fact, seem virtually indistinguishable from hypotheses. Consider this one, for example: "People have killed animals since the earliest times, and used the fur, bones, etc., for various purposes" (*OC* 284). This looks very much like it could be tested according to historical evidence and justified on logically prior grounds. There are all sorts of things which would have to be the case if it is true, and having spelled out these truth conditions we might look to see if they are fulfilled by the available facts. Animals would have to have existed since ancient times, their remnants would have to show signs of human labor, their death would have to be attributable to human causes, etc., etc. There is no single condition to be checked here, and much of our evidence might be indirect. Yet there seems to be no reason why we could not gather such evidence and therefore no reason why we could not treat this claim as a hypothesis. The only odd thing about checking the truth conditions of such a claim is that the factual evidence to be used in its support is no *more* reliable or *more* certain than the claim in question. Anyone who doubts this assertion could just as well doubt any of the facts brought forward in its defense. Thus one could describe the claim as a hypothesis only in the barest formal sense of the word; it has independently specifiable truth conditions, and these conditions can be independently assessed, but they provide no better footing for its rational grounding. Here the resort to evidence is *possible* but otiose. This could be disputed if one could show that the evidence of unnatural death among animals in ancient times is more certain than the fact that people sometimes killed them; but then we could just as well switch the example to the claim, "Animals have lived and died since earliest times." We could assign truth conditions to this belief, too, by spelling out its entailments; but we would not arrive at any more *secure* level of judgment by recasting the issue in this way. *That* kind of independence, which characterizes the truth conditions of a hypothesis, is missing in the truth conditions of these beliefs.

There are other certainties, however, which we cannot even begin to treat as hypotheses. In the case of direct perceptual judgments, for example, we cannot resort to evidence because we cannot even *specify* independent truth conditions for these judgments. The truth of these judgments has nothing to do with evidence. Rather, the truth of immediate perceptual judgments is determined by the proper use of the terms involved. Thus if I say "this paper before me is white," I cannot spell out any further truth conditions by which this claim might be tested against an independent set of facts. To say what must be the case if this claim is true, I can only say that *the paper must be white*—that *p* here must be the case if "p" is true. I cannot recast the issue in any more primitive propositional terms, as if it could be decided on logically prior grounds; so I cannot treat the claim as a hypothesis. Yet I can be mistaken if I do not understand the meaning of "white," or if my vision is impaired due to some sort of unusual circumstance. Judgments of this sort, therefore, can be doubted—only the doubt is not removed by checking their various entailments against the facts. The doubt is removed by checking one's usage against that of other competent speakers of the language and by checking to make sure that the visual circumstances are normal.

Principles, by contrast, do not fit either of these last two categories. They are not so certain that the resort to prior grounds and independent evidence in their defense would be superfluous. They often need a defense, but a defense on independent grounds is not possible. It is not possible in the case of immediate judgments of sense, either; but then principles are plainly not *immediate* judgments. Immediate perceptual judgments apply so directly to particular items of sense experience that we cannot break their truth conditions down into any more primitive terms. Principles, on the other hand, are implicitly *general* assertions, and they have a whole range of particular entailments. If these entailments could be independently checked against the facts, principles could be confirmed or disconfirmed. Yet the truth conditions of a principle cannot be corroborated *without the prior assumption of the principle's truth*, and they cannot be contradicted *without the prior assumption of its falsity*. Principles, therefore, lack the *independent testability* of hypotheses, as well as the *immediacy* of perceptual judgments.

The only kind of proposition which principles resemble is a third type of certainty, a type which includes assertions such as "there are physical objects" and "there are colors" (*OC* 35, 57). One of Wittgenstein's interpreters calls these truisms "methodological propositions," but Wittgenstein himself hesitated to describe them as *propositions* at all.[4] At one point he said that they were just nonsensical, since there are no circumstances in which it would make sense to *propose* such things (*OC* 35-36). Who would these claims inform, and how? Believing in physical objects or believing in colors is not a matter of holding opinions but a matter of commanding rudimentary conceptual capacities—knowing how to locate things, to describe them, to distinguish one from the other, and so on. The development of these capacities and the "belief" in physical objects go together, so that there is no need whatever to assert such a thing once one has mastered these various linguistic skills of referring and describing. Rather, we use the concept of a physical object and the concept of a color to make formal distinctions between types of reference (e.g., to physical instead of immaterial objects) or between modes of description (e.g., by color instead of other properties). Given the capacity to make these distinctions, it serves no added purpose to say that physical objects and colors exist. Nor can we suspend the capacities which go into such distinctions, as if we could discuss the belief in physical objects or colors *without* relying on the usual means of identifying and describing objects. We have no other ways of talking.

The reason why one might call such assertions "methodological," therefore, is that they reflect linguistic capacities which we cannot do without. We cannot imagine any context in which new evidence would give us a reason for doubting the existence of physical objects or colors. Using evidence to manufacture doubts requires the same underlying capacities for referring to various objects, describing them, and categorizing them, etc. Here we "believe in" physical objects and colors by the way in which we use our language, and we cannot continue to use it intelligibly by suspending these beliefs. Certainties such as these are too deeply ingrained in the rudiments of our speech; by the time we know enough to question any hypotheses they are beyond debating.

Principles are also, in a sense, "methodological" propositions. One believes or disbelieves in a principle according to the way in which he operates—in the kind of judgment he makes, in the concepts he uses, in what he counts as a good judgment, a relevant reason, and so on. And because an adherence to principles affects the way in which we interpret, or categorize, our "evidence," we can no more verify a principle on evidential grounds than we can defend the belief in physical objects by pointing to a few examples. The resort to evidence in both cases *presupposes* the belief in question. Both types of belief have entailments, in other words; but to check these entailments against the facts one has to exercise the same conceptual capacities which are incorporated in *belief.* Simply to point out a physical object is to believe in the

II

42

existence of such things, and the same is true of principles — to point out favorable evidence is *eo ipso* to believe.

This does not mean that principles are certainties, however. It simply means that principles and "methodological" certainties both lack independent truth conditions. Beyond that there is an important difference. The conceptual capacities presupposed by certainties of this kind are so rudimentary as to be virtually indispensable in learning a language, whereas the conceptual capacities involved in the mastery of principles represent additional ways of explaining or interpreting that which we can already describe in rudimentary ways. While there is no point in asserting something like the existence of physical objects, therefore, there is a point to advancing a principle. Principles add new discipline to one's thinking. The concepts which they incorporate fit over our experience in new ways, in ways designed to bring an entire range of phenomena under a *supervenient* form of understanding. That, in fact, is why it often makes sense to say that we believe, not in various propositions, but in certain *concepts*. When matters of principle are at stake, the belief in key concepts and the affirmation of explicit propositions represent alternative ways of saying the same thing — that our experience is subject to an added dimension of understanding.

One can see what I mean by taking a familiar example. "Nature," we say, "is uniform in her ways"; and we accept this claim as a fundamental principle of scientific inquiry. It is not a perceptual judgment, though, for nature is not a discrete object which we observe to have a certain observable property, uniformity. The term "nature" covers a whole range of phenomena, and the property "uniformity" indicates something which is common to all these phenomena without being immediately apparent in any. In effect, the principle that nature behaves uniformly says that any natural phenomenon can be understood as an instance of a regular pattern; and by positing this as a general ideal, this principle provides the norm and warrant for explaining natural events in terms of *natural laws*. Thus, one who subscribes to this ideal of scientific explanation could just as easily say that he believes *in the concept of natural law.* Either form of affirmation casts an ideal of explicability over an enormous range of our experience. For again, the principle of nature's uniformity states (1) that all natural phenomena are subject to a given form of explanation, and (2) that this type of explanation can be reached by conceiving these phenomena as instances of natural law.[5]

This belief in the uniformity of nature is not indubitable. We know that there are people who do not share it, and we know that it can be shaken by recalcitrant phenomena, such as psychic phenomena or subatomic events. It is only indispensable to the pursuit of one type of explanation, and we could give up this type of explanation without unravelling the whole fabric of our language. Yet such a belief does not have to be absolutely indispensable to be reasonably reliable, and the belief in the uniformity of nature is certainly reasonable in this sense. We expect every reasonable person with a modicum of education to accept it as a regulative ideal of scientific inquiry.

Unlike scientific *hypotheses*, though, this belief cannot possibly be verified or falsified. We cannot verify it by direct observation, since it does not assign any perceptible characteristics to any particular thing. And we cannot verify it indirectly as a hypothesis, since there is no way to check its entailments against independently known facts. To say what must be the case if it is true, one can only generalize about natural phenomena, saying that this one and that one and every other one must be explicable in terms of natural law. If natural law explanations could be firmly established *without* presuming the very thing which we wish to corroborate, nature's uniformity, there would be no problem in this. We could present every known instance of natural law explanation as evidence in favor of the general claim that nature behaves in a strictly law-like way. Yet we cannot know that natural laws are invariant—i.e., that they are *laws*—unless we already know that nature is uniform, yesterday, today, and tomorrow. There can be no natural law explanations where there is no uniformity.

The problem in treating this belief as a hypothesis is not

that it has no specifiable entailments or truth conditions, but that its entailments cannot be independently verified. Nor can they be falsified. A single counter-example might disprove it if it were a general hypothesis; a single inexplicable natural event would be sufficient. The inexplicability of a natural event, however, is even harder to establish than its explicability, since the absence of a ready explanation for any particular event may be due to our own ignorance, not to any inherent opacity, irregularity, or inexplicability in nature. Of course, if we *know* that nature follows no regular course in one of her regions, then we can be sure that natural law explanations for events in that domain will never be found, no matter how much more we learn. That is not something we can independently know, though, and so we can only beg the question by building the falsity of this principle into the presentation of counter-examples.

Principles, in short, are both indemonstrable and indefeasible on evidential grounds. They regulate further judgment by postulating ideals to which these judgments are to conform, and they fix these ideals by binding their subjects and predicates together in a *definitive* way. This does not immunize principles against the force of anomalies and apparent counter-examples, but it does affect the way in which principles are defended — and this is important. Consider, for example, the principle that nothing vanishes without a trace. To maintain this belief as a matter of principle, one must hold fast to it as a definitive ideal for monitoring change. Whatever vanishes *must* leave traces; that is part of what it means for something to have an objectively real existence. Or to put it another way, one must be able to find the traces of a vanished object *in principle*. The phrase "in principle" here reflects the fact that not-vanishing-without-a-trace has been built into the concept of a "thing," so that one would have to alter his concept of existing things to deny the principle. Even so, there may be pressure to do just that. Thoughts often seem to vanish without leaving any traces, and so do clouds and rainbows and various other things. To maintain the principle in the face of these counter-examples, one has his choice of two lines of defense: he may treat the counter-examples as merely apparent anomalies, or he may restrict the *scope* of the principle to a narrower range of relevant examples. In other words, he may say that thoughts and clouds and the like *do* leave traces when they vanish (though we are not always able to find them); or he may say that the principle, though obviously a generalization, is not meant to cover *everything*. Perhaps it applies only to physical things, so that thoughts and images do not count against it.

Any principle can be defended by restricting its scope. The property which it assigns throughout its domain is an *essential* property, so that the possession of this property coincides with the extent of the principle's application. Thus, any principle which can be read forward as a generalization, so to speak, can also be read backward as a definition. The principle of nature's uniformity, for example, can be read as the generalization "everything natural is lawlike"; or it can be read as the definitive claim, "the lawlike is (by definition) the natural." This second, explicitly definitive, way of reading the claim reflects its role as a principle; for that is how the ideal of natural law explanations is held in place — by making this kind of explicability an essential property of every *natural* phenomenon. At the same time, the definitive quality of the principle makes it possible to defend the belief in uniformity (lawlikeness) by excluding recalcitrant phenomena from *nature's* domain. Something like this seems to be happening in subatomic physics. Apparently the behavior of subatomic particles cannot be monitored without interference, so that their individual movements cannot be traced. For all practical purposes, the behavior of these particles, taken individually, presents itself as random or lawless activity. Of course, some unknown law might still operate on this level; and one could defend the belief in uniformity by holding out for this possibility. But one could also defend the belief by restricting it to events on a larger scale, setting aside subatomic events as *subnatural* events, much as religious believers set aside other events (i.e., extraordinary coincidences, miracles, etc.) as *supernatural* events. Such a principle, after all, need not have an *unlimited* domain.

Nevertheless, one pays a price for defending his principles by narrowing their scope. By ruling apparent anomalies out of bounds, one sacrifices the comprehensiveness of his principles, and the credibility of a principle heavily depends on its comprehensiveness. General hypotheses die by counter-examples (unless they are propped up by auxiliary hypotheses), but principles only wither away in their scope until they are replaced by more powerful principles. Hence, it is preferable to maintain the scope of a principle by reducing all threatening anomalies to the form of explanation which that principle anchors. When this is not possible, these anomalies will accumulate; and as they do, it will become harder and harder to maintain the principle's credibility. It may never be *disproven*, but it may be effectively replaced.

When such principles are replaced, they cease to function as definitive generalizations. The conceptual ties which held these principles in place as ideals of explanation fall apart, so that the entailments of these claims can be checked without begging the question of their truth. This not only relieves a superceded principle of its regulative role but also exposes it to falsification. The relaxation of these ties has to occur first, though; no principle can be treated as a falsifiable hypothesis as long as it serves as a *definitive* truth. A new ideal of explicability has to be introduced by a new principle before an old principle can be discarded.

Psychological inquiries, for example, can be launched from a number of different perspectives defined by a number of different principles. According to one school of thought, all human behavior represents an attempt to reduce anxiety. According to another, all behavior is the product of operant conditioning. The adoption of one or another of these positions commits the psychological investigator to treating every instance of human behavior as being susceptible, "in principle," to the appropriate form of explanation. Thus one committed to the first principle must stretch the notion of anxiety to make it fit every type of behavior. One who relies on the second principle, however, need not insist on anxiety as an omnipresent motive of human action. Since he has another form of explanation to invoke, he can afford to treat the claim that all behavior aims at anxiety reduction as a hypothesis. From *his* point of view, this claim no longer plays a definitive role in psychological inquiry and can be given up to falsification.

The same thing happens in economic science. Many economists base their forecasts and explanations on the assumption that rational well-informed people always act to maximize their own utility. Others disagree, and apparently with good reason. Many people seem to mismanage their goods, squandering their money, allowing their property to depreciate, neglecting various profitable investments, and so on. Still, the advocates of this principle are loath to give it up, since it establishes (for them) the fundamental form of economic explanation. Thus they take great pains to protect this claim from counter-examples. People who do not manage their affairs to maximize their utility do not qualify as rational agents, and the aberrations which they cause in the economy are said to wash out when the big numbers come in for the economy as a whole. Or such people are said to maximize their interest in goods which have no value for the rest of us. As long as economic inquiry depends on the belief that our behavior must be motivated by the desire to enhance our economic interest *if it is to be economically intelligible,* economists must explain these anomalies simply to preserve the possibility of economic science. Yet if this founding principle of economics can be superceded by another — e.g., by the principle that people endeavor simply to *maintain* their economic power — then economists can cease to define reasonable agents in terms of an insatiable will for more goods. They can admit that some reasonable and well-informed people do not always attempt to maximize their own utility, since they no longer have to adhere to this claim *as a matter of principle.* Instead, they can relax their hold upon it, letting it subside to the level of a general hypothesis subject to telling counter-examples.

In any case, the logical status of the proposition itself, isolated from the role which it plays in economic inquiry, is ambiguous. It can be read as a general hypothesis or as a principle, and its falsifiability depends entirely on this feature of its logic: it must be read as a hypothesis before it can be abandoned to counter-examples. This can happen to any principle which anchors a domain of inquiry by fixing its key concepts in definitive, regulatory, ideals. If the subject matter of that domain can be reconceived, so that its problems may be submitted to another form of explanation or interpretation, the principles which once informed the search for solutions can be given up as *definitive* truths — or, indeed, as truths of any kind.

Adding this last point to the previous contrasts and comparisons, we can outline the basic differences between principles and other kinds of assertions. Principles say what they say about the world by attributing some form of explicability or intelligibility to a whole range of phenomena, thereby founding a regulated order of inquiry or a disciplined domain of interpretation. Their truth or falsity can never be directly ascertained because these attributes are never immediately apparent. Nor can their truth or falsity be indirectly determined on evidential grounds; for as long as they continue to serve as regulatory ideals, the assumption of their truth will affect the interpretation of their "evidence," making it impossible to assess their truth on independent grounds. Principles can only be frustrated by phenomena which resist the form of explanation which they underwrite; they can never be falsified in a decisive way by independently known facts. Their conceptual role simply precludes any telling determination of their truth.

None of this means that principles cannot be reasonably held, however. It simply means that we cannot expect to answer our doubts about them in the same way in which we justify and defend hypotheses. Principles are prey to serious but ungrounded doubts about the cognitive value of the whole range of judgments which they inform, and their credibility depends in large measure on the possibility of overcoming such doubts. This is vitally important to remember when we come to religious principles and to the vexing problem of their justification. They too may be reasonably held, but only as other principles are held — through a kind of faith, buttressed more by the understanding which follows from them than by the evidence which underlies them.

2

Before taking a religious example, however, we need to make a few more distinctions. The term "principle" has so many variants and near relations in common usage—"principles of judgment," "rules," "formal principles," "laws of logic," etc.—that we need some finer distinctions to cut through the confusion this jungle of terminology creates. By sorting these things out, we can considerably sharpen the sense in which religious assertions conform to the logic of principles.

These distinctions are all the more important because the crucial question of the cognitive significance (the possible truth) of religious claims depends on the specific categories to which we assign them. It makes all the difference, for example, whether we regard them as purely *practical* principles having nothing to do with *knowledge,* or whether we construe them as *theoretical* principles having something to do with genuine *understanding.* Unfortunately, however, this distinction between practical and theoretical principles suffers from so much ambiguity and confusion that it offers us little help in the analysis of religious assertions until some prior distinctions are in place. It simply reflects the difficulties we face.

To sort through some of these difficulties, suppose we start with the difference between principles—in the sense in which I wish to use the term—and *rules.* Since principles all serve some kind of regulative function, it is tempting to think that they must be rules of a very general sort. In fact, we do use the term "principle" to characterize rules of utmost generality. Yet I think that it would be a mistake to identify all principles with rules, as this would obscure the difference between principles which have an *assertive* force and principles which are merely regulative. Rules, after all, are never true or false. Rules are purely prescriptive; they define or delineate permissible practice, and thus they can just as well be expressed in the form of generalized imperatives as in the form of indicatives. One can state a rule of chess, for example, either by saying (in the indicative) "the bishop moves only along the diagonals of its original square," or by saying (in the imperative) "move the bishop only along the diagonals of its original square." These two formulations are virtually equivalent; nothing in the indicative is lost in transition to the imperative. Principles, however, cannot always be converted into imperatives without a change of sense or loss of force. Principles *seem* to be convertible into generalized imperatives simply because they have a regulative aspect. Thus, in maintaining the uniformity of nature, it looks as if we could just as well say what we mean by using the imperative expression, "treat every natural phenomenon as an instance of a regular pattern." But this imperative lacks the force of saying that nature is in fact uniform. It could be a stipulation based on some arbitrary fiat, whereas the indicative is a *postulate*. The imperative here, in other words, is actually a *derivative* expression, conditioned by an underlying truth claim. It means, "if you want to *understand* natural phenomena, then treat each one as an instance of a law-like pattern."

In short, the fundamental principles that we use to ground our efforts to understand the world always *posit* something, and to this extent it makes sense to think of them as truth claims. But rules, again, are never true or false; they are only useful or useless, acceptable or unacceptable, required or superfluous, and so on. Admittedly, there are certain cases — morality, for example — in which it is hard to tell whether our rules are derived from principles in this strict sense or from more general rules called "principles" and based on convention. Yet this does not mean that the distinction between rules and principles is vacuous; for it makes a difference whether we regard a moral principle, such as the claim that human beings are ends in themselves, as a disguised prescription or as a moral truth claim. It makes a difference in the kind of justification which we allow it to have, and it makes a difference in the kind of force which the moral life assumes for us. If it is only a rule, then appeals to authority or considerations of practical utility might be enough to justify it. If it is a principle with assertive force as a truth claim, however, authority or practical utility will no longer suffice for its justification; and the pursuit of the moral life, like the pursuit of truth itself, will appear as an end in itself, incumbent on every rational creature.

In any case, we need to preserve some distinction between truth claims with rule-like roles to play and rules themselves. This is far wiser than treating every normatively significant assertion as if it were only a disguised prescription, for some of these regulative assertions do in fact say something about the world. They say that it calls for explanations or interpretations of a given sort, and the role which they play in defining these patterns of explanation depends on these claims.

Statements of principle, therefore, should not be confused with *rules of inference*. Rules of inference are prescriptions which define what inferences or logical transformations are permissible in valid arguments. They never supply the *premises* of an argument because they are not truth claims to begin with; they simply tell us how the truth of an argument's premises can be preserved in its conclusion. Principles, on the other hand, do provide premises for arguments. From the principle that every event has a cause we can infer that any particular event has a cause, but the rule of inference which justifies this conclusion (universal instantiation) guarantees only the form of the argument. The scientific principle about events and causes supplies its substance.

We need a similar criterion to distinguish between *formal* and *material* principles. Formal principles have no particular content and consequently impose no substantive restrictions on the judgments which follow from them. They are not field-specific or limited to any particular area of inquiry. Rather they define the universal conditions which must be met by judgments in any field. Thus the formal principle that a proposition and its denial cannot both be truth is definitive for all propositions, regardless of their content. Similarly, the principle that every value judgment must be generalizable identifies a definitive feature of all *normative* claims. Material principles are just the opposite; they are field-specific. They delineate the ideal form of our explanatory judgments by defining the way in which the subject matter of these judgments is to be conceived.

Furthermore, formal principles, since they do not assert the need for any particular form of judgment, do not really say anything about the world. Because they define *propositions*, they are *necessary truths*, or truths which must hold in all possible worlds. They are not assertive principles, or *postulates*, at all, as they could not possibly be false. Rather they belong to the "laws of logic." Substantive principles, by contrast, can be false. The principle that every event has a cause would be false in a world where everything happened by chance; and the principle that people tend to maximize their own utility would be false in a world (possibly this one) in which people endeavored only to *satisfy* their needs. Our world, after all, does not always *yield* to the kind of explanation which our principles underwrite. The principles which we cling to often lead us to expect understanding in a form in which it is not available, so that our inquiries, being framed in accordance with these principles, are continually frustrated by inexplicable anomalies. When that happens, we eventually conclude that our principles are false, even though we cannot disprove them.

The only trouble with this is that it distinguishes material, substantive principles from formal principles and from rules without telling us if there is any essential difference between *fundamental* principles and other *principles of judgment.* Presumably, fundamental principles are more "basic" than principles of judgment, but this difference could be a difference in kind or a difference in degree. Of course, our normal habits of speech do not always reflect clear distinctions; and in this case I am inclined to think that ordinary usage leaves the distinction between fundamental principles and principles of judgment ambiguous. One can take it either as a qualitative distinction in kind or as a relative distinction of degree.

Any principle, insofar as it governs the kind of judgments we make, can be described as a principle of judgment. In effect, every principle is a principle of judgment, simply because every principle exerts some regulative force on the judgments which follow from it. Some principles, however, have a much wider scope than others; so we might contrast the relatively more general from the less general by saying that they are more "fundamental." The principle of sufficient reason, for instance, has a broader scope than the principle of nature's uniformity. It asserts the potential explicability of virtually *everything*, not just natural phenomena but freely willed behavior, historical developments, subconscious anxieties, religious conversions, etc. The principle of nature's uniformity applies only to natural phenomena, yet it covers a wider range than the principles of any particular *branch* of natural science, such as the chemical principle that matter is neither created nor destroyed in a molecular reaction. Here we have only a difference of degree, and we might describe those principles of greater scope as being more fundamental than those of lesser scope.

As a difference in kind, though, the distinction between fundamental principles and principles of judgment is more interesting. Consider, for instance, these two principles of aesthetic judgment: (1) "good literature possesses an inherent value apart from its moral or practical utility," and (2) "a good novel must have a coherent plot." The first seems more fundamental because it is broader in scope, yet the difference between the two goes beyond that. The first not only differentiates aesthetic values from moral and pragmatic values, it *posits* these values and implicitly asserts the possibilities of some nonmoral, nonutilitarian, kind of judgment. The second does not; it tells us instead how to go about making this kind of judgment in a particular area of criticism. In other words, the fundamental principle (1) says that aesthetic judgments are possible, while the principle of judgment (2) supplies a criterion for it. And since the truth of (1) is a necessary condition for the applicability of (2), it makes good sense to say that it is fundamental. One who denied (2) might still believe (1), but one who denied (1) would have no use for (2).

If the difference here still seems unclear, consider the case of natural science again. We have principles of induction, such as those formulated by J. S. Mill, to guide us in the search for causal explanations; but there would be no need for these principles if nature were so chaotic that it made causal explanation impossible. Mill's principles, or "canons," of scientific method rest on the prior assumption that nature is *not* that disorderly

II

and that causal explanations can be traced through uniform laws of nature. The more fundamental principle, therefore, is the one that posits the explicability of natural phenomena and founds this dimension of understanding. Everything else depends on that.

With these last points behind us, we can return to the troublesome distinction between *theoretical* and *practical* principles, perhaps the most confusing of all. This distinction is clearest (and least controversial) if "theoretical" simply means *scientific* (empirical) and "practical" simply means *nonscientific* (nonempirical), for then one can invoke the distinction without suggesting that every practical principle is merely a rule. Then nothing inherent in the use of these terms forecloses the possibility that some of these practical principles might also, in some sense, *be true*. Yet the term "theoretical" is often taken as a synonym for "cognitive," so that the contrast one draws between theoretical and practical principles does double duty by excluding practical principles from the domain of *possible* truth. Worse yet, the notion of cognitivity usually goes hand in glove with the notion of empirical testability; so on the one side theoretical principles, empirical hypotheses, and cognitive claims all tend to coincide, while on the other side practical principles, empirically untestable assertions, and noncognitive utterances begin to coalesce. This so *loads* the distinction between theoretical and practical principles that it creates more controversy than it helps to resolve.

Positivistically inclined philosophers *want* to say that theoretical principles concern matters of fact, while practical principles concern only normative questions of behavior. Yet this begs the question of whether or not truth is at issue in the "practical" judgments of morality, or in the "higher" judgments of religion. So far I have suggested that truth claims are involved wherever our principles tell us that the world is subject to certain forms of explanation or evaluation, something which would not be the case if the world were radically different than it supposedly is. This reflects a very broad notion of truth claims, and it may sound strange to those who are philosophically accustomed to identifying truth claims with empirically testable hypotheses. Nevertheless, I think that the broader notion is more justifiable and in Chapter IV will argue the point at length. Meanwhile, we can assume that truth claims are assertions with significant denials. They say something about the world which could be true in some possible world (presumably this one) or false in some other possible world. To ascribe truth and falsity to principles, therefore, we need only to make sense out of the possibility that the world we live in makes a difference to their credibility.

In other words, we need to make sense out of the possibility that *some* world might not yield to the kind of explanation or interpretation which truth-bearing principles support. I think that we can do this, not so much by imagining particular empirical givens to be different than they are, but by imagining more and more of the same sort of anomalies that already threaten our principles. Such anomalies do not decisively disprove a principle, but they exert some pressure on it; and that is enough to show that there is a connection between what a principle asserts and the way the world is. Some principles fit more easily over our experience, leaving fewer anomalies in the way of belief. Others must be forced, stirring up recalcitrant phenomena on every side. The former we have more reason to regard as true, the latter more reason to suspect of being false.

Given this way of handling the true/false distinction, we can handle the theoretical/practical distinction however we like. Whether we say that every practical principle is only a noncognitive prescription and every theoretical principle a truth claim, or whether we distinguish practical from theoretical principles according to the *kind* of truth claims involved, makes little difference — as long as we are clear about what we are doing.

Such clarity is particularly important wherever religious beliefs are involved. The role these beliefs play as truths to live by, the kinship they bear to certainties, and their peculiar susceptibility to groundless doubts all suggest that they are principles. But are they practical principles or theoretical principles? If one says that they are practical principles, this is apt to imply that they are not truth claims. Yet if one says that they are theoretical principles, this will invite confusion with scientific principles or with metaphysical speculations. Neither of these unguarded views is adequate. Religious beliefs are principles that are full of practical import but that also bear some relation to *truth.* They are *truth-bearing* assertions, and to that extent, theoretical claims; but they are also *regulative* assertions, and to that extent, thoroughly practical claims. They are truths to live by, *which could be true.*

If any substantive religious principles *are* true, however, the truths which they represent are not the sort of facts which lie open to empirical investigation and scientific discovery. The substance of religious claims does not come from given facts about the world around us, but from the order and intelligibility — the *sense* — which can be discovered in these given facts. Religious principles, that is, are second-order claims, claims about the way in which one set of truths (the known facts of nature and of history) can be comprehended under another aspect (according to their reason for being or their ultimate purpose). To those who think that every truth or every fact must be fundamentally alike, it must seem strange to postulate such higher truths, existing beyond what we would ordinarily call the realm of facts. Yet religious are not the only assertions which force us to recognize a different order of truth claims. Every substantive principle bears the same supervenient relation to given experience, since every such principle grounds a form of explanation or interpretation in which we submit known facts to another, higher, kind of scrutiny.

Principles, to put the point figuratively, are like lenses that we fit over our thinking to raise it to new powers of discernment, not simply to magnify or to multiply the facts before us but to disclose other intelligible aspects of our experience. We do this, for example, when we say that human beings have free will; this then becomes the lens through which we focus on human behavior in terms of motives, rationales, excuses, and so on. Or we say that human beings have inalienable rights;

then this becomes the lens through which we appraise our political life in terms of justice and injustice. Or again, we say that we are biochemical organisms; this becomes the lens through which we look for scientific explanations of our activity. All of these claims are matters of principle, for they all tell us that human experience is subject to one or another form of understanding. Yet none of them can be checked directly against the facts visible through lenses of a lower power, the lenses we use for rudimentary descriptive purposes. Rather, we believe in such principles by *using* them to search our experience; and for those whose understanding is increased by this kind of focused inquiry, these beliefs stand fast as fruitful assumptions.

All this is as true of religious principles as it is of any other. They too represent lenses through which one can draw one's experience into a different focus, and their reasonableness depends on their power of illumination. Inasmuch as they tell us that our experience calls for judgments of some sort, grounded in the ideals that they postulate, they "say something about the world." What they say cannot be spelled out in terms of direct observables, nor can it be indirectly verified through evidence. Yet the difference that their truth or falsity makes shows up in the understanding we derive from them. Religious principles help believers to organize, to interpret, or to make sense out of their experience, and to this extent they can be reasonably held. Or they fail to do this, and for that reason can be justifiably rejected. Here reason requires only that our principles be true enough to yield *some* increase in *some* form of understanding.

3

Measured by the standards which apply to principles in general, therefore, religious principles might be as true and as credible as any other substantive principles. This possibility, though, depends on the *need* for religious principles, for there would be no point in maintaining religious principles if there were no distinctively *religious* type of understanding to be gained by religious reflection. This type of understanding must be recognizable as such — as *understanding*, not just subjective fancy. Otherwise, if there were nothing unusual about the kind of judgment that religious questions require, or if religious questions were pseudo-questions, there would be no need for religious postulates to frame a new order of judgment. One could dismiss religious reflections altogether, or one could handle religious questions by extending some other form of inquiry in accordance with some other principles — e.g., by turning scientific inquiry toward the solution of existential concerns.

The scope of scientific inquiry, however, is obviously not that broad. It leaves moral problems, for example, quite unsolved, so that we have to postulate some moral principles to raise our thinking beyond the level of natural fact to questions of right and wrong. That is how the moral aspects of our behavior are disclosed and submitted to judgment. Similarly, if logic is to hold any place for religious principles, those principles too must be needed to raise the level of our thinking to the pitch of some higher concerns, untouched by other realms of thought. Not just science but every other disciplined form of inquiry must leave religious questions unanswered, so that a dimension of understanding remains for religious postulates to disclose. Yet what kind of understanding is this? What sort of questions require a peculiarly *religious* response?

Not all believers articulate their concerns in the same way, of course, and one should beware of generalities on this point. Religious judgments vary so much in their form and content that common characteristics are hard to find. Nevertheless, I think that it is fair to say that such judgments commonly deal with finitude, fate, death, suffering, and other universal human concerns. The *type* of judgment needed to address these concerns, broadly speaking, is *teleological.* The questions to which religious beliefs typically speak — and which other forms of inquiry leave untouched — are questions about the meaning and end of existence; and the principles that underwrite this kind of thinking are generally postulates about some purposeful order in or "behind" all that is. Indeed, if I had to formulate the most basic, minimally religious belief, I would say that it is the principle of sufficient reason interpreted teleologically: things have a *reason* for being. Sheer existence, with all its mysterious givens and disturbing contingencies, must have some higher rationale, some end that renders individual existence worthwhile and capable of fulfillment. This is the theme on which the world's religions play their different variations. The point of postulating a higher order in the cosmos is to legitimate the individual's search for a worthwhile end in his own existence; and the point of conceptualizing this order in a particular way is to direct the believer to that end, so that he might live with the sense that he is passing his life for the best.

We can generalize about religious belief in this way because of the comparable role which religious principles play in bringing the inescapable conditions of human life under a supervenient form of interpretation. The actual content of these doctrines varies — indeed, it varies so widely that one cannot find any common denominator in terms of specific dogmas. Not everyone who is religious believes in God, for example. Nor does every believer think that history is moving toward a divinely appointed culmination. Yet it is hard to imagine any religion that does not promise the kind of satisfaction which comes from living in accordance with *some* higher order. Thus, in one way or another, religious principles vouch for a worthwhile ground or end in all that is, thereby enabling believers to pursue a meaningful existence under the assumption that the needful understanding is available. Fate, arbitrary suffering, and death all fulminate at the center of religious concern because they force us to look for this kind of higher rationale. Why should such things be? And how are we to live with any measure of affirmation or satisfaction in the face of them? By assigning some *raison d'être* to life in general, the central teachings of a religious tradition hold out the warrants which the believer needs to pursue teleological judgments in the midst of all the apparent contingencies which envelop us. And by laying down the possibility of these judgments through a conceptually fixed ideal, these doctrines regulate the believer's thinking by defining the pattern to which it must conform. We therefore have every reason to call these beliefs "principles" and to seek their peculiarly religious nature in the kind of thinking which they sponsor.

One can see what I mean by taking the doctrine of divine creation as an illustration.[6] This teaching, though it is often advanced as a theory of how the world came into being, actually belongs to a teleological order of judgment in which it functions as a first principle. Admittedly, it looks like a causal explanation for the world's existence, as if it were meant to satisfy our curiosity about how there happened to be a world in the first place. Unlike every other scientific or quasi-scientific explanation, though, this one is not a claim to natural fact or to anything comparable to natural fact. It tells us why there is a world—because God created it; yet the kind of answer which this represents is not the kind of explanation which natural causes can provide. To say that the world is the creation of a divine being is to say that it has a reason for being in the teleological sense, not a reason for being in the sense of a particular causal origin.

This last remark may sound controversial in the light of the usual Judeo-Christian picture of a mighty being calling the world into existence out of the void. Yet if one construes such an image of creation along the lines of a naturalistic explanation, as if it offered a supernatural parallel to causal explanations of a scientific sort, the *point* of attributing the world to God would be utterly lost. Every naturalistic explanation accounts for one given (the effect) in terms of another (the cause), so that the search for natural causes never moves outside the realm of the contingent, or that which is given "by nature." Hence, even if the connection between a natural cause and its effect exhibits the necessity of a natural law, the fact that nature operates according to this or that law simply represents *one more given* within the world as we find it, all of which comes to us as a *brute* reality. Those who are religiously concerned, however, do not need to know any additional brute facts of life so much as they need to know whether these contingencies can be absorbed in a higher perspective or whether they reflect the absence of any meaningful end in existence. Here it does no good to trace the brute facts which pose this problem back to prior contingencies by means of naturalistic explanations, nor does it do any good to trace these facts to *super*natural givens lying beyond the range of empirical knowing. It does no good, that is, unless the point of invoking a supernatural explanation is to go beyond contingent matters altogether and to posit some teleological ground of being — which is just what the doctrine of divine creation does. It posits the existence of God as the *raison d'être* of all that is, so that the sheer givenness of natural existence can be encompassed, in principle, by thoughts of purpose. This is not a liberal way of reading the creation "theory"; it is something which no *religiously* significant account of the doctrine can afford to give up.

One could just as well say, therefore, that the doctrine of divine creation actually *is* a teleological claim. It has to be. Since there is no set of contingencies from which ultimate purposes might be deduced, all derivative judgments of purpose have to be grounded in assertions which are themselves teleological. Merely to get the religious search for meaningful ends off the ground, to pursue judgments of purpose as if there were purposes to be discovered, we need principles which tell us that the world provides for this kind of thinking. That is what the doctrine of creation does. Rather than adding to our perplexity about the givenness of all that is, it answers this perplexity by saying that the world has its reason for being in God. This then shifts the believer's thinking onto a supervenient level of judgment in which he directs his thinking toward the discovery of God-given purposes. The belief in divine creation effects this shift because it presents the world of nature as something which is endowed with purpose by a supremely intelligent being — by a God who acts *intentionally*. When the believer extends this idea to the contingencies of his own existence — his fate — he begins to look for the meaningful end which his own creaturely status must entail. He does this in accordance with other religious teachings which color his outlook and shape his expectations, so that his judgments actually reflect a network of regulative beliefs. Yet none of these judgments of purpose would follow from the belief in divine creation unless it were a teleological principle to begin with.

This, in fact, is why God *by definition* must be a transcendent being. Inasmuch as our questions about the world's reason for being inevitably take us beyond questions of natural fact, the belief in a creator God could not possibly answer these questions if the existence or nonexistence of God were construed as a natural—i.e., brute—fact. God could not just happen to exist, or the fact of his existence would leave the why and the wherefore of contingent existence just as perplexing as it was before. Asserted as a natural fact, the existence of God would no longer ground the givenness of all things in a source of purpose; and thus it would no longer say anything about the meaningfulness of our individual lives. God, therefore, must be a *super*natural, or transcendent being, not because he must be located somewhere beyond the edges of space where we cannot discover him, but because the assertion of his existence must extend beyond contingencies into the realm of purpose. *The supernatural character of God,* in other words, *is simply the counterpart of the supervenience of teleological judgment.* The point of placing God metaphorically outside or above the domain of nature is to make it clear that the question of his existence belongs *outside* the "logical space" of contingent claims.

For the same reason, the doctrine of divine creation cannot be reduced to the question of a "first cause." One can, if he likes, eliminate every personalistic description of God and use the term as a synonym for "uncaused cause" or something of the sort. And one can argue for the existence of such a stripped-down God, but he cannot expect to sustain a religious view of the world merely by winning this argument. Shall we assume a first cause?—so far this is only a question of adding or not adding another being to the long list of all that is. Yet the addition of one more entry on this list, even if it is "necessary being," would not ground contingent existence in a *religiously* satisfying way. It would merely tell us that we must assume a first cause along with all the other causes, giving us no assurance that the whole sequence serves any higher purpose. Therefore we could still ask, and would have to ask, whether the existence we share with all other beings has any potential for fulfillment.

I know that it sounds somehow reductive to say that religious assertions about the existence of God or the creation of the world are really only statements about the world's susceptibility to a certain kind of interpretation. This seems to overlook the "ontological" or "metaphysical" side of religious belief. Does not the doctrine of divine creation depend on the actual existence of a *being*, an objectively real God with real properties, however dimly understood? Such a question is perfectly understandable, but it makes the suggestion that religious claims function as teleological principles seem more dangerous than it is. I am not saying that religious claims have nothing to do with reality, or that they bear no relation at all to prevenient questions of fact. Rather, religious principles postulate teleological grounds for judgment *by way of asserting ontological or supernatural realities.* Thus, to say that there is a God is to say that there *really is* a meaningful ground to existence; for that is the point of insisting on the ontological side of religious belief. It is just that one cannot take such a claim in two parts, first the *bare* question of God's existence (the ontological question) and then the added question of purpose. The ontological aspect of belief here simply *qualifies* the teleological postulate as a *truth* claim. We refer to God as a being, in other words, to indicate that truth is at stake in adopting a religious view of the world. And I agree with that. Yet this truth cannot possibly be extracted in the form of neutral kernels of metaphysical fact since the teleological implications of such a belief determine its *sense.* To see that sense and to get at this truth, one has to work *through* teleological judgments, not around them.

This explains why believers who are anxious to maintain the metaphysical reality of God are also anxious to retain the anthropomorphic descriptions associated with the "God of religion." These descriptions protect the belief in God from misunderstanding by making the teleological import of believing in God stand out. If God is a being with intelligence and will and compassion, then his creation must be a product of intent, filled with purpose. We are not to take this anthropomorphic idea literally, no doubt, but neither are we to take it lightly. We are not to take it literally because the point of such a teaching is not to describe anything which we might *discover.* The belief is not that kind of factual claim. Rather, the anthropomorphic formulation of the belief in God helps to convey the idea that the world around us has a meaningful ground and end *whatever the unknown natural facts of its origin may be.* As causal or quasi-scientific accounts of the world's beginnings, therefore, the believer can reject anthropomorphic descriptions of divine creation. He need not hold any opinions at all on this question, nor even believe that the question makes sense. He only has to believe that questions about the world's *purpose* make sense, and that the world is so constituted that at least some of these questions can be answered when they are pursued in the form suggested by the anthropomorphic language of his principles.

If I am right about all this, then those who approach the doctrine of divine creation as if it should be spelled out more fully as a plausible account of the world's origins are making a big mistake. This doctrine does not explain anything in the sense of a scientific explanation and does not intend to. It certainly does not reduce the mystery of the world's existence to an instance of natural law, nor does it advance our knowledge on some deeper metaphysical level. Viewed as an explanatory hypothesis, it simply substitutes one mystery (the existence of God) for another (the givenness of all things) without producing any net gain in understanding. The term "God" merely takes the place of that unknown explanation which we do not have but which we posit on the strength of the (perhaps overextended) principle that everything has a cause. The world, we think, must have come into being somehow, so we simply draw up an entity to fill the bill of a causal explanation and call it "God." This no more advances our knowledge or our understanding than the naming of any unknown. It merely restates the need for an explanation in the form of a stand-in solution.

Yet again, the doctrine of divine creation does not purport to explain the mystery of contingent existence, as if the mystery of it all might be removed by postulating a supernatural cause. It fills the need for an explanation in another way—by vouching for the world's intelligibility on a higher level in terms of its meaning and ultimate worth. In this respect the doctrine of divine creation is no different than the principle that nature operates uniformly: the latter does not explain any general feature of the world's existence, it only vouches for the possibility of explaining particular events according to a certain ideal. The doctrine of divine creation does the same thing, only the ideal varies. The principle of nature's uniformity vouches for scientific explanations according to natural law, while the doctrine of divine creation vouches for teleological explanations according to the will of God.

NOTES

1. *The Encyclopedia of Philosophy*, ed. Paul Edwards (New York: MacMillan, 1967), contains no entry under the heading of "principle," and the term does not even appear in its glossary of logical terms.

2. Hypotheses are not always completely verifiable or falsifiable, since their truth conditions cannot always be exhaustively checked. Moreover, they can usually be saved from falsification by adding or subtracting subsidiary hypotheses to change their entailments. Nevertheless, the facts by which we test hypotheses must be independently ascertainable if we are to speak of verification or falsification at all. This is a strictly logical point about the necessary conditions of objective testing. It says nothing about the necessity of *empirical* tests.

3. Thomas Morawetz develops this point in another way in *Wittgenstein and Knowledge* (Amherst: University of Massachusetts Press, 1978), chs. 2 and 3, especially pp. 43-45 and 74.

4. Morawetz, *Wittgenstein and Knowledge*, pp. 38-40.

5. Admittedly, this is a simplified account of the belief in uniformity, since the principle can be interpreted in subtly different ways—e.g., as a claim which supports only absolutely invariant laws or which includes statistical generalizations. Yet the general point still stands: principles say what they say about the world by postulating a form of explanation appropriate to it.

6. By "the doctrine of divine creation" I mean something which is found in theistic religions generally, not a particularized version found only in one religious tradition.

III
PREDESTINATION
AS A TYPICALLY
RELIGIOUS BELIEF

Sometimes a broadly sketched idea seems more appealing at a distance than it does under close examination, but the idea that religious assertions generally function as principles is just as appealing in its detail as in its rough outline. Given only a general view of the nature of principles, one can see that religious claims require the same kind of commitment — or *faith* — which any principle demands. Since fundamental principles can never be securely grounded in evidence, one who believes *in* them must rely *on* them as axiomatic assumptions, trusting that the insights which follow from them are weighty enough to hold them in place. Religious principles, in this respect, are no different from any other principles. Yet there is more to the comparison of faith claims and principles than this. The closer one looks at the logic of principles the easier it is to see that the special kind of commitment which faith claims require is due to a special aspect of their sense — their point. A principle acquires its point by virtue of its regulatory role; and when this aspect of its meaning is misunderstood, the attempt to affirm it degenerates into a pointless form of mere assent.

Looking more closely at the logic of religious principles, however, means looking at an example; and the more commonly misunderstood the point of a particular belief is, the better example it is likely to make. By rescuing the point of such a belief from misunderstanding, the difference between affirming the belief *as a principle* and assenting to it as a *pointless hypothesis* can be dramatically illustrated. The claim that God predestines his elect to eternal happiness or to eternal damnation is just such a belief. Even for those who understand and appreciate other Christian teachings, it is hard to know what to do with this one. It is notoriously offensive to nonbelievers and exceedingly difficult to defend. Many Christians, I suspect, simply ignore it; others disavow it. A few try to soften the harsh impression it makes by qualifying it, by adding further claims about God's foreknowledge, and so on. Yet this perplexing doctrine takes on a new aspect when its regulatory role as a religious principle is understood. Then one can see the point of the doctrine, and one can see how a faithful adherence to such a belief depends entirely on a grasp of its point.

1

To those who know the doctrine of predestination only as a thorny dogma that seems to undercut both the justness of God and the free will of his creatures, it may come as a surprise to learn that Luther thought of this teaching as a great comfort—indeed, as "the Christian's chief and only comfort in every adversity."[1] On the face of it, this doctrine seems far more frightening than comforting, since it is terrifying to think that one might be arbitrarily excluded from salvation by divine fiat. If this is how it is, then there is little difference between the God of Christianity and the personified Fate of paganism. Such a God makes all of us the victims of an arbitrary destiny, a destiny which seems unspeakably cruel to those who through no fault of their own are left to misery and damnation. Unless, of course, God somehow foreknows the virtues of his elect; but in that case God's foreknowledge seems to close our futures in the stifling grip of determinism. How can God know what people are going to do in order to reward or punish them in advance of their deeds, if it lies within their power to do as they please? Or if it does not lie within their power, how can they be said to be worthy or unworthy of his grace? And how can God be said to be just in dispensing this grace?

Perhaps there are answers to these questions, yet the abstruse metaphysical maneuvers needed to reconcile predestination with divine justice seem like desperate attempts to neutralize an embarrassing element of Christian tradition. Luther, by contrast, was remarkably unembarrassed by the doctrine. This was not because he was blind to the problems which we see, but because he approached the doctrine from such an entirely different direction that he treated such problems as misunderstandings. To worry about them was beside the point. Thus, just as Paul brushed aside the thought that God's grace might be enhanced by our sinning (Romans 6:1), Luther dismissed as a misunderstanding the use of predestination as an objection to divine justice.[2] He made no metaphysical attempt to reconcile predestination and divine justice. To have done so might have made the doctrine more credible in a superficial sense, but it would not have made it any more edifying as a truth to live by. In fact, it would have done quite the reverse by evacuating its point.

Seen in the light in which it was preached, the doctrine of predestination turns out to be much less threatening than it seems. Essentially it is a doctrine of grace; as such it belongs in the context of debate over the role of good works in attaining salvation. In that context, the claim that salvation comes by prior election represents an emphatic denial of any kind of *merited* acceptance before God, or "works righteousness." Certainly Luther saw the doctrine in this light, and the great comfort he found in it was plainly due to the way in which this teaching relieved him of the burden of having to fulfill certain prerequisites for receiving God's grace. He had been taught that God's grace was freely available, but only to those who were properly repentant. Only those who sincerely and completely confessed their failings, and who sincerely willed to live according to the law of God, would be forgiven and strengthened. For them the sacraments would be the ever-available means of grace, but for those who lacked or lost a purely receptive heart, the sacraments would become ineffectual. Now, at first glance, this seems fair enough; if divine favor is a gift which is not distributed wholesale, then it should at least go to those who deserve it. Anything else would be arbitrary and unjust.

Yet Luther found only severity and despair in this understanding of God and His grace. The harder he tried to achieve a pure and contrite heart, the more acute his conscience became; for in devoting himself to righteousness he learned more of sin than of grace, until he felt nothing so strongly as the inner corruption of original sin. The problem was that he could not create within himself the pure heart that he thought God required; the more he tried, the more conscious he became of an inner disharmony between the self he willed to be and the self he was. He wanted to feel a spontaneous love of God and a natural desire to do God's will, so that he might be assured of receiving the grace which Christianity had promised. But one cannot force oneself to have a *naturally* good will. The effort expended in being natural and spontaneous is worse than wasted, as it simply increases one's consciousness of *not* being good by nature. Thus, in his effort to become pure in heart Luther was like one who on some grievous occasion tries to feel appropriately saddened, but in *trying* to feel sad feels only unnatural and insincere. Only the man who tries to force his sadness feels hypocritical for a time, whereas Luther felt altogether lost in an endless cycle of despair. The more he struggled to purify his will, the more hopeless the task became; and the more hopeless the task became, the more angry he became with God for imposing such an impossible condition. That in turn made him feel even more impure, more lost, and more angry, until he "raged with a fierce and troubled conscience."[3]

Given that state of mind, one can easily appreciate Luther's relief when he began to see in Paul's Epistle to the Romans an entirely new conception of divine mercy and grace. From the point of view of a sinner struggling with a wayward will, the

III

72

requirement that one revive a *naturally* pure intent was too severe. The God who demands this is a God who chooses to bestow his grace as a consequence of human merit, even though the merit here is only a matter of intent and not of actual works. Indeed, this is just what grace comes to on this account; God makes up the difference between what we intend and what we actually accomplish in the way of doing his will, so that we can actually *achieve* the righteousness needed for salvation. One's intent, however, must be pure to begin with if God's power is to bring it to fruition; and as Luther discovered, it is every bit as difficult to be pure in heart as it is to be pure in deed. No, it is even more difficult, for if there is one thing which people might feel obligated yet helpless to be, it is to be pure in heart. A system in which God grants his grace according to the reformation of a sinner's intent would constitute a fair arrangement — more than fair — if only people could meet this initial condition. If they cannot, as Luther came to feel, then God's mercy and justice look more like wrath and cruelty.

How different this all becomes if there are no conditions for grace, if God holds forth His forgiveness with no strings attached. If salvation comes by *election*, as the doctrine of predestination implies, then the oppressive task of purifying the will disappears. God grants His grace prior to anything the sinner does to earn it or receive it, so that it remains only for one to believe in it and to be grateful for it. From this point of view, the doctrine of predestination does more to support the justness and mercy of God than it does to impugn it. What appears to be a harsh teaching takes on an entirely different aspect when juxtaposed with a sinful consciousness, for so long as God offers His grace *in consequence* of the believer's merit, the acutely conscious sinner is left without hope. If God grants His grace *prior* to the sinner's hopeless attempts to rectify his impure will, however, then the happiness which he could not possess through his own effort becomes possible through God.

Ironically, this seemingly frightful doctrine of predestination provides new hope for those in despair by bringing to light a completely transformed conception of divine mercy. Instead of a God who is merciful because he treats his creatures *fairly* according to their success in measuring up to certain standards of worthiness, the doctrine of predestination presents us with a God who is merciful because he releases his creatures from conditions that they cannot fulfill. To renew the possibility of salvation, he takes salvation out of the sinner's hand, so that it has nothing to do with rewards and just desserts. Hence it would be beside the point to judge his doctrine of predestination according to the usual notion of fairness. The point of the doctrine is to *displace* the idea of fairness and just rewards in connection with the problem of securing one's happiness, since the idea that God grants unhappy people his grace as a consequence of their worthiness to receive it is one which leads in practice to despair.

The logical insight to be gained from this is that the doctrine of predestination depends on the context in which it is preached and received. It presumes a sinful consciousness and all the attendant difficulties of coping with the inner disharmonies of despair, and it carries its comfort only to those who understand it in this connection. Outside this context of personal concern the doctrine loses its focus; its point disappears, and it stirs more anxiety than it quells. No one knew this any better than Luther himself, and he cautioned against giving such "strong wine" to those who were not yet ready for it. To be of "due maturity," he said, one must first feel the weight of his sin in order that he might recognize this teaching as a doctrine of grace. To struggle with the idea of predestination in any other way can only bring hurt to ourselves and anger toward God.[4]

This is not only good theological advice, it is also very instructive from a philosophical point of view. A religious belief, like the doctrine of predestination, acquires its point—its fine focus, as one could say—only in its proper context. Out of context, its implications become unfocused and its point becomes obscure. Not only does its comforting aspect disappear, its very *sense* changes; so that it no longer carries the same consequences for those who affirm it. After all, one can understand every word used in a doctrine's formulation and still misunderstand the point of believing in it; and so the

III
———
74

wording of such a belief is not enough to insure every aspect of its interpretation. That is why people can differ so sharply in their attitudes toward predestination. Even though the words are familiar to all, some do not see the point of the doctrine. They lack the contextual backing needed to appreciate the proper implications of the issue.

The relationship between context and belief here is subtler than it seems. In one sense, the implications of an assertion always vary according to the assumptions which one brings to it. Implications of that sort, however, are derived by an external inference, whereas the point of a religious belief is an internal matter, independent of the various implications which can be derived from it in conjunction with other propositions. The point of the doctrine of predestination depends on the role which it plays in reordering the judgments one makes in the pursuit of happiness, and the import that the doctrine acquires through this role comprises an inherent aspect of its meaning. Thus, the *role* that it is intended to have determines the implications that it is allowed to bear.

If it seems peculiar to talk of assertions having roles, we should remember that various beliefs occupy different logical rungs in our thinking. Some of these beliefs, such as testable hypotheses or bits of information, have little or no role to play in determining our *patterns* of judgment. Other beliefs, namely principles, do affect these patterns; they define the ideals to which they conform. Thus the concept of a contextually dependent assertion should be much easier to understand if we think of principles rather than hypotheses. A principle belongs in a certain context because it has a *scope*, a limited field of judgment in which it applies. It acquires its point by virtue of the role it plays as a governing ideal in that field. The principle of uniformity of nature applies to scientific inquiry and grounds the ideal of natural law explanations. The principle that human beings have rights applies to moral and political reflections and informs our deliberations about obligation, and so on. Outside its proper context, each would lose its point despite the familiarity of its wording. The doctrine of predestination is no different; the fact that it owes its point to a certain context simply shows that it too functions as a regulative assertion.

Like other religious beliefs, the doctrine of predestination informs that order of judgment in which we try to encompass our existential concerns with thoughts of purpose and meaningful ends. Luther and his theological opponents all believed in a God who endowed human beings with an ultimate end, thereby making them heirs to the prospect of perfect happiness and fulfillment. They all believed that this end (salvation) could only be reached through the grace made available to them through the life and death of Jesus. Thus, when they came to argue fine points about divine election, grace, and good works, they were a long way from arguing the kind of fundamental principles through which teleological orders of judgment are instituted. Yet even in these upper reaches of Christian reflection, the beliefs at issue still made a difference in the way in which the prospect of fulfilling one's end was to be pursued. Seeing the point of the doctrine of predestination, therefore, was not simply a matter of recognizing it as a doctrine of grace; it was a matter of *reorienting* the effort to reach one's end and to secure one's happiness.

That is why Luther warned against drinking from this cup too soon. If one imbibes the doctrine before having the appropriate problems to go with it, then he will not discover any comfort in it as an affirmation of God's grace. Worse yet, his profession of faith will go unaccompanied by the changes in thinking and living which this doctrine is supposed to instill. When that happens, believing becomes literally pointless and faith degenerates into mere assent. Having missed the point of the doctrine, the believer cannot *comply* with his belief. Even if he becomes somehow *convinced* about its truth, he cannot reorient a way of thinking which he has not yet begun. To be of "due maturity," he needs to have become sufficiently frustrated in the search for happiness that he sees in this teaching a new way of continuing. Then, when believing will make a fundamental difference in the way he pursues his happiness, he is ready for such strong wine.

2

This last point about faith and mere assent is too important to pass over lightly. The acceptance or rejection of a doctrine like that of predestination makes a difference not only in one's attitudes and religious affections but in one's thinking and practice; and this difference is the measure of the believer's faithfulness—i.e., of his compliance with the regulative implications of his principles. The difference between a compliant faith and an empty profession of belief, though, can be a subtle thing. It may not emerge in any obvious behavioral changes. To see what it involves, we need to take a closer look at the belief in predestination and the changes which it might or might not make in a person's inward life.

It is tempting to think that the belief in predestination should not make any difference at all in one's life. Lifted out of the faith/works context and presented as a hypothesis, the claim that God predestines us to happiness or unhappiness looks like a brand of metaphysical determinism. And it looks as if the consequences of accepting or rejecting it should be about the same as they are for other versions of determinism—which is to say that they should be about *nil*. Suppose that it is such a hypothesis. As long as it remains unconfirmed, a reasonable person will want to protect against the possibility that it will turn out to be false; so this person cannot abandon the effort to secure happiness through his own power. On the other hand, the doctrine might also be true; but in that case it does not seem to matter much what one does, since his fate is already sealed. One might as well go on struggling to attain those ends which would bring happiness, then, *regardless* of his opinion on this subject. Any other strategy would be foolish. It would be foolish, that is, if it made any sense to think of the doctrine of predestination as an unconfirmed hypothesis.

Yet that cannot be the proper way to understand this issue. Construing the doctrine of predestination as a deterministic hypothesis simply evacuates its point, leaving us with a caricature of faith. For even if one firmly believes that his fate *is* sealed by God, it is not clear that he should change the way he lives. Should he cease all efforts to attain his happiness? Or should he simply do as he pleases, now that his fate is out of his hands? He could do either, and either would be equally compatible with his belief in determinism. He could do anything, thinking that it does not matter what he does, or thinking that his "decisions" are in some way made before he arrives at them. Here the point of believing is so unfocused that the issue dwindles to insignificance.

One does not have to be a nonbeliever to misconstrue the doctrine in this way. A believer who accepts the doctrine as an established fact—out of the blue, so to speak—faces the same uncertainty about its implications. Say that a believer accepts the belief in predestination because he finds it in scripture, which he takes as an unquestionable criterion of truth. How does he know what to make of it? Where does he fit it into his thinking? Should he continue his attempts to please God, or should he abandon himself to his inclinations? Or should he not seek some sign of his election, so that he will know whether he has been listed among the chosen or banished with the damned? Once the believer has the doctrine established for him as an opinion which he must hold, he cannot help but wonder what its implications are. Nor has he any clear way of telling, for when the doctrine is detached from its role as a principle, the dutiful believer is forced to profess it—to give his assent—without knowing how to abide by it.

The most disturbing thing about this is that the doctrine can remain unfocused in its implications even when it is confined to the faith/works controversy. In that context one can see that predestination rules out any attempt to earn one's happiness through one's own efforts. But does that mean that the believer can abandon "good works" altogether? The most logical thing to do might be to accept one's ultimate fate, whatever it might be, and to spend the remainder of one's life trying to secure as much earthly happiness as possible. Yet that understanding of the doctrine has never been acceptable to Christian theologians. The point of the doctrine is not to instill a *moral* fatalism, as if the pursuit of a virtuous life and the fulfillment of one's obligations no longer mattered. That too is a misunderstanding.

Rather than destroying the believer's sense of moral and religious obligation, the doctrine of predestination *conditions*

III

those obligations by incorporating them into a higher perspective. It puts these obligations in a new light by changing the way in which the believer relates his ultimate well-being to his successes and failures *as a moral being*. In his own inner court of judgment, where he examines himself according to his worth, he changes the sanctions that he attaches to his judgments. Instead of punishing himself with absolute condemnation for his moral failures, instead of hoping that he were not the self that he is, he relies on the belief in predestination as a means of escaping such inward alienation. By believing that God's "election" precedes his own good works, he gives up his *sovereignty* as a final judge of his acceptability and worth. That makes it possible for him to accept himself *without* thereby condoning his failures or relaxing his moral ideals.

This, at least, is how the doctrine of predestination should be interpreted if Luther's understanding is at all representative of the Christian tradition. Luther's sense of insincerity in trying to force a good will drove him into a state of self-alienation from which there seemed to be no escape. He could not relieve the inner discord of a sinful conscience because he treated the purification of his will as a prior condition for his own acceptability. This condition, by its very nature, could not be fulfilled by forcing oneself into a better moral disposition. His attempts to make himself worthy by rectifying his will simply made him feel more artificial, driving him deeper into despair over himself. Desperately, he tried to prove his worth through an arduous show of righteousness and monastic piety; but that produced only self-deception instead of self-acceptance. He was too anxious to prove himself because he was too acutely aware of his imperfect will. Yet he could not give up the attempt to become a better person because his ability to accept himself depended on some evidence of his moral worth. To give up without that evidence would be to accept defeat as a human being, permanently foregoing any hope of inward, lasting, happiness.

The only other alternative would be to turn defiant, remaining in sin out of spite; and Luther may have come close to that when he raged against God for making even the slightest virtue so hard to achieve. Yet the angry attempt to mock one's conscience, or to stick fast in sin out of spite, does nothing to restore a peaceful conscience; and so that kind of willful self-assertion will not bring happiness either. The only hope of overcoming such a divided conscience is to remove the burden of moral achievement so that one does not have to reject his moral ideals or to hide his moral failures in order to accept himself.

Christianity removes this burden through the promise of divine forgiveness. A whole network of teachings convey this promise, doctrines about atonement and grace as well as election. Together these teachings tell the person who is trying to prove his worth that he has no right to hold himself against himself according to his own conditions of self-acceptance; God has done away with those conditions by accepting the sinner in spite of his sin. In the light of this acceptance, the believer's moral shortcomings remain, and he remains painfully aware of them; but he no longer has to pretend that these shortcomings are incidental to his better nature in order to maintain his integrity. He need not hide from himself in a deceptive display of righteousness, or salvage his pride by making a show over his high moral standards and his inability to forgive himself. Believing that God has found him acceptable, he can afford to acknowledge his impure heart and imperfect nature as his own. He can dare to *be* himself, not in the sense in which he turns himself over amorally to his inclinations, but in the sense in which he gives up the hopeless attempt to make himself acceptable unto himself.

Dispositionally, this represents a type of resignation. The believer surrenders the attempt to show himself to others as a morally deserving individual. Having nothing which he must hide from himself or from others, his willingness to "confess" becomes the sign of his belief, and his openness toward the help he receives from others becomes a symptom of his new-found security. This brings no ensuing relaxation of his moral duties, however; only his approach changes. Instead of trying to fulfill his moral obligations for the sake of his own self-acceptance, he tries to fulfill these obligations out of gratitude.

These obligations give him the opportunity to repay the unwarranted acceptance which he feels has been bestowed upon him, and so he no longer resents them as the cause of an inner disharmony between the self that he is and the self which he would have himself to be. At least, this is supposed to happen. When it does not—when one professes his belief in divine forgiveness without undergoing any change in his disposition—then such a believer either does not understand what he believes or does not really believe.

Now to say that some such dispositional change must accompany religious belief, rightly understood, is unlikely to stir much controversy. But how and why this is the case—the logic of the matter—is not so clear. Perhaps religious assertions are merely psychological means for bringing about certain changes in attitude. Perhaps belief *as such*—i.e., belief in the *truth* of these teachings—is unimportant. This, no doubt, is a logical possibility, although those who hold such views have yet to explain how a belief can serve its proper function without being maintained as a truth claim. Ordinarily, we would say that a believer must maintain the truth of a doctrine such as that of divine forgiveness if he is to take any psychological comfort in it. If he were to hold this doctrine in the sense of *entertaining* it as a psychologically useful idea, it would not effect any telling changes in the way he judges himself. In fact, it might only perpetuate a divided and self-deceptive consciousness. By telling himself that the doctrine of forgiveness performs a useful psychological function, someone at odds with himself over his guilt might try to use the doctrine to promote his self-acceptance—without actually believing that he is forgiven. That would not solve the problem of his guilt; it would only cover it up by making it appear less serious than he knows it to be, in which case the point of the doctrine obviously will not be served. No, the believer has to think that he has in fact been released from the hopeless task of proving his worth; and that means that he must believe the doctrine of divine forgiveness has some truth in it.

That is not the only reason for resisting a purely psychological account of religious belief. The changes which religious principles bring about are more than attitudinal shifts. When one adopts the belief in divine forgiveness or divine election, a change in thinking accompanies the inward relaxation of the believer's disposition. He brings his judgments about himself, his plight as a human being, and his prospects for happiness into line with a new pattern. He continues to think that his happiness consists in doing the will of God, not in selfishly exercising his own will; and since he sees the moral law as a public expression of God's will, he continues the effort to fulfill his moral obligations. Thus, nothing so drastic as a departure from moral principles follows from the adoption of the additional doctrine of predestination. Yet his thinking does change. The belief in divine election supervenes the judgments which the believer makes about his moral obligations, drawing the whole business of trying to fulfill God's law into a new perspective. *Rather than thinking that his ultimate happiness and fulfillment might be secured as the end-product of moral achievement, the believer foregoes the whole range of means/ends judgments in connection with his happiness.*

The difference which this change of principle makes is remarkable. We usually associate happiness with something which we can directly pursue, such as financial success, a love relationship, better health, and so on. This makes it possible for us to think of happiness as something which we might achieve, for we can direct our efforts toward these various ends expecting happiness to follow their attainment. When this way of thinking about happiness is extended to the moral life, the moral law takes on the appearance of a means to the end of happiness, as if happiness could be achieved by fulfilling all our moral obligations. Moral virtue, from this point of view, becomes the condition which must be satisfied for the attainment of a larger aim; one expects his happiness to follow as a consequence of his moral endeavors. Christianity often seems to encourage such expectations by promising heaven as the reward for fulfilling the moral law of God; but in reality the central teachings about divine grace, election, and forgiveness do just the opposite. They encourage the believer to think of

III

happiness in a completely new way, not as something which can be achieved by pursuing deliberate means to a definite end, but as something which comes by way of resigning the attempt to make oneself happy. Thus, one who believes that his salvation — i.e., his ultimate happiness — has been provided by grace as a kind of gift no longer sees the moral law as a *condition* for his own happiness and self-acceptance. The law, instead, becomes the means by which he might express his *gratitude*. With that his inner life changes. Instead of struggling against himself to fulfill the demands of his conscience, or condemning himself for his imperfection, he takes up his life with a new peace of mind, welcoming his moral obligations as a chance to repay his happiness.

To those who do not think about their happiness in such religious terms, the believer's peculiar way of regarding his happiness seems imprudent. He takes too little care to avoid suffering and misfortune, he exerts too little effort to attain worldly goods, and, worst of all, he *counts* himself as a happy person even though he has done nothing to deserve it. None of this makes any sense to one who thinks of his happiness as something to be engineered, nor is there any reason why it should make sense from that perspective. The believer's conception of happiness and its attainment is so different from the ordinary prudential conception that his standards of what is reasonable or unreasonable to do as a self-concerned human being differ from those of nonbelievers. As long as happiness lies within our power to achieve, it is unreasonable to neglect the means of its attainment; but if happiness can only be had by resigning the attempt to manufacture it, then it is unreasonable to pin one's hopes on worldly achievements, even on moral achievements.

The fact that the adoption of religious beliefs about divine forgiveness and election produces such a thoroughgoing change in the way believers think about happiness shows that principles are at stake here. To believe in these teachings, one must understand their point and abide by their regulative implications, and that requires more than a change of attitude. It requires a change in judgment, a change in the way one conceives and pursues his happiness and a change in the way one determines his own self-acceptance. That is why the test of a believer's sincerity and understanding in affirming a religious belief is the use which he makes of it in reordering his thinking as well as his disposition. The affirmation of a hypothesis, since it always develops within an unquestioned framework of judgment, never requires such a fundamental change; and the affirmation of a religious belief *as* a hypothesis never brings such a change. To have faith, in a Christian doctrine or in any other religious principle, one has to change the way he assesses his life. He has to adjust his sense of what finally matters in human life, and he has to bring his prospects of fulfillment under a new rubric of understanding. Otherwise, the mere profession of belief will be pointless, and the insights to be gained by making these changes will never be realized.

Unfortunately, the fact that we commonly distinguish articles of faith from less consequential issues does not insure their proper understanding. People still get these beliefs out of context, they still miss their point, and they still try to judge them without knowing what it would mean to think in accordance with them. Hence, when a particular teaching goes chronically unaccompanied by the changes which should attend its adoption as a principle, theologians usually reformulate it or add some corollaries to it, thereby expanding and complicating a religion's body of doctrine. The doctrine of predestination, in fact, plays just such a correlative role in support of the more fundamental doctrine of divine grace. To make it clear that grace cannot be earned, and thus to displace the working assumption that happiness is to be attained by pursuing means to some definite end, salvation is said to come by way of *election*. Then to make it clear that *election* cannot be prudentially managed, God is said to have chosen his elect "before the foundations of the world were laid." Instead of minimizing misunderstandings, though, this can just as easily multiply them; for the point of it all can still be missed. Those who still think of happiness as an attainment, or as a reward for moral efforts, can become extremely anxious over the thought that God has already passed out the rewards. Wanting to know whether they will receive one of these rewards, they may begin to seek signs of their election. Then, as they grow more desperate to secure their happiness, they may try to manufacture these signs of election, as if they could convince themselves that they were slated for happiness in a life to come — whereupon self-deception takes the place which should be occupied by a new approach to happiness. In one final attempt to eliminate this misunderstanding, faith itself — i.e., a sincere trust in God's grace — is said to be the one sure sign of election. But, of course, that too can be mimicked in bad faith. The point of it all can still be missed.

In view of all this misunderstanding, it is hard not to wonder if the doctrine of predestination has not done more harm than good in protecting the point of Christianity's central claims. If predestination simply represents Christianity's way of saying that genuine happiness does not come as a direct consequence of our efforts to attain it, and that self-acceptance cannot be engineered, then one ought to be able to reformulate the doctrine in a less misleading way. Perhaps one could retain the point of the doctrine simply by saying that the grace by which we are able to live at peace with ourselves is given *logically*, not *chronologically*, prior to our efforts to attain it. This would still block the fruitless attempt to procure one's happiness by trying to recreate oneself from the bottom up, starting with an impure will. And it would still prevent anyone from *crediting* his acceptability to himself. At the same time, such a simplified version of the doctrine would eliminate the misleading picture of God arbitrarily separating the elect from the damned prior to creation, so that one no longer would have to posit God's foreknowledge of human merit in order to salvage the belief in his justice.

3

We can leave it to Christian theologians, however, to decide what reformulations of the doctrine of predestination preserve its point. Meanwhile, there are some other philosophical problems to attend to. A doctrine like that of predestination acquires its point by virtue of the role it plays in reorienting the judgments a believer makes about himself and his prospects for happiness. Assuming that one understands all this, just how is he to justify such an extraordinary belief? Or is justification too much to expect? This is the sticking point to which any honest account of faith must eventually come.

If there were some convincing way of defending the belief in predestination, this problem of justification would be relatively easy to handle. One could simply proceed with its justification and let that stand as a model for the justification of other religious claims. Yet there is no convincing way of justifying this belief. Like other religious principles, the only evidence which a believer might offer in its defense comes saturated with assumptions which the nonbeliever does not share. Instead of using this doctrine as an example of a justifiable religious belief, one would do better to use it as an illustration of the difficulties involved in defending religious assertions. Then, at least, the problem can be clarified.

We tend to think that the reasonable thing to do is to wait until the truth of a belief can be established before acting on it, and for the most part this is good advice. If we did not dispassionately evaluate the grounds for holding a belief before acting on it, we would all too often deceive ourselves, thinking and living in accordance with assumptions which turn out to be false. This is such an elementary, commonsensical rule of thumb that it mesmerizes us, leaving us inattentive to exceptions. We cannot expect to test every belief in advance of holding it, since some assumptions are needed as the conditions of our reasoning, and they are not subject to demonstration.

The belief in predestination is one of these assumptions. It is plainly not an empirically testable hypothesis; for even if one could somehow distinguish the elect from the damned, he could not know whether the elect were eternally chosen prior to their merit or rewarded in consequence of their faith. It is a supervenient claim, designed to subsume facts which we already know under a new rubric of interpretation. Thus, if it is testable at all, it seems more reasonable to treat it as a

III

86

metaphysical claim, judging it by the abstract criteria of consistency, economy, and comprehensiveness. That has been the traditional approach of philosophical theologians. To make the doctrine more credible as a metaphysical hypothesis, they have tried to reconcile the belief in predestination with the belief in divine justice and in human free will, thereby rationalizing all these beliefs by systematizing them.

Since assertions of any kind have to be consistent to be jointly true, one can hardly blame theologians for this. Yet it is one thing to defend one's beliefs against the charge of inconsistency, and it is quite another thing to advance positive grounds for thinking that they are true. To expect speculative considerations to ground religious assertions and promote religious belief is to expect too much. Indeed, if one makes systematic considerations his only grounds for belief, as if the religious claims at issue were accepted or rejected solely on the basis of their coherence and comprehensiveness, he will violate the logic of good judgment just as surely as he would if he tried to verify his religious principles as empirical hypotheses. The mishandling of religious beliefs in this case is more subtle, but it is mishandling nonetheless.

Suppose, for example, that a theologian clears away the usual objections to the doctrine of predestination by explaining how God, without depriving human beings of their freedom and responsibility, might choose his elect *fairly* through a foreknowledge of their merit. Given such an account, those who object to the doctrine as a threat to divine justice and human freedom no longer have any reason to complain; and as a result, the doctrine itself begins to look more reasonable and more believable. Yet in leaving the question of truth for speculative criteria to decide, one severs the essential connection between the doctrine and the regulative role which gives it its point. In this case, God's justice is upheld by making human merit logically prior to election, and election temporally prior to human activity — but what comfort remains in that? The concept of election becomes pointless, as one's happiness on this view is still something which one earns through his own efforts. Practically speaking, one might as well say that God rewards the virtuous believer and leave it at that. Here one simply emasculates the doctrine of predestination by attempting to justify it in a way which pays no attention to its role as a principle.

The same holds true of principles in general: *one can never afford to justify them by criteria which they are meant to supplant or supervene.* Consider another example: suppose someone who knows very well how to make prudential judgments doubts that we have any moral obligations whatsoever, and that he insists that we justify our fundamental moral principles by showing how their adoption would promote his self-interest (e.g., his health, or pleasure, etc.). "A reasonable person always acts out of self-interest," he says; "that is just what being *reasonable* means." Clearly, as long as the point of moral principles is to override such prudential considerations by instituting prescriptive judgments of *obligation,* the moralist cannot afford to defend his principles on his opponent's grounds. The moral believer would defeat his own purposes if he set aside the point of his principles merely to win their acceptance on prudential grounds, for the acceptance of these principles as prudent policies would not require the believer to exercise any higher ideals. Such a believer would not enter into any *new,* peculiarly *moral,* domain of judgment. Without adhering to moral beliefs as the foundation for a different kind of reflection, beyond prudential reasoning, he simply would not become a dutiful person. And for all those who believe that we have moral duties, that makes no sense at all.

Thus, if being *reasonable* in matters of religious belief means treating religious principles in a similar way, ignoring their role in instituting higher forms of judgment, then it is no wonder that Luther spoke of "killing reason" to make room for faith. Yet if being reasonable means treating an assertion in accordance with the logical function which it is meant to serve, then Luther may not have been so irrational. Too often the seemingly rational attempt to justify religious beliefs within the framework of some nonreligious system of judgment promotes their credibility only at the expense of evacuating their point.

Luther did not do that. Disputing other theologians, he appealed to scripture in defense of predestination; but his faith ultimately rested on the new vista of understanding which opened up when he grasped the point of this belief and took it to heart. Any other way of "grounding" this belief by detaching its credibility from the role it plays as a principle would have been completely illogical.

The possibility of holding reasonable or appropriate religious beliefs, therefore, cannot be solved by showing what sort of objective or independent grounds might be used to justify them. When the governing principles of supervenient forms of reflection must be weighed, one cannot satisfy his doubts about these principles without some idea of what is to be gained through their adoption. Religious principles are advanced as the logical means of assessing the ultimate worth or the point or the acceptability of our lives, and they implicitly promise to deepen our understanding if we conform to them. If some are truly promising, however, this is something one must learn for himself. This is not peculiar to religious belief; it is hard to see how anyone might become reasonably confident about the uniformity of nature, for example, without entering into scientific inquiry and seeing how well it proceeds on this foundation. The same could be said of the governing principles of morality, or depth psychology, or aesthetics, although the "findings" in those areas of judgment will naturally be very different from empirical discoveries.

These findings will be different in the case of religious beliefs, too; in fact, they will be so different that it is hard to explain what a peculiarly religious finding might be. Perhaps one might find himself in the sense of being able to accept himself and to consolidate his efforts to live a meaningful life. Perhaps he might find some sense or order in what once appeared to be an arbitrary life history. And perhaps he might offer these insights as testimony for the governing principles through which he views his life. Yet the "insights" and "findings" which believers claim in defense of their principles might also be read *into* their experience rather than read *out* of it, so that it makes no sense to speak of these principles, or the judgments which follow from them, as being right or wrong, true or false. If that is how it is, then religious claims must fail as reasonable assertions because they fail first as intelligible assertions. If they do not really say anything about the world, they neither need nor permit any justification as truth claims.

Having returned to this point, however, there is little more to be gained from the example of predestination. The question of whether or not this belief, and others like it, have anything to do with truth is as much a question about the concept of a truth claim as it is a question about the nature of religious claims. And there is no point in pursuing the possible justification of religious claims until we have secured a better idea of what a truth claim is.

NOTES

1. Martin Luther, *The Bondage of the Will*, in *Martin Luther*, ed. John Dillenberger (Garden City: Anchor Books, 1961), p. 185. I have chosen a Lutheran account of this doctrine without worrying about its Christian orthodoxy. The orthodoxy of his view is debatable, of course; but that does not affect its philosophical value as an illustration of religious belief.

2. *The Bondage of the Will*, Dillenberger, p. 200.

3. *Preface to Latin Writings*, Dillenberger, p. 11.

4. *Preface to the Epistle of St. Paul to the Romans*, Dillenberger, p. 32.

IV
ARE RELIGIOUS BELIEFS TRUTH CLAIMS?

In practice we speak of religious beliefs just as we do of other beliefs, as assertions which might be true or false. What seems commonsensical in practice, though, often seems dubious upon reflection, and the use of "truth" and "falsity" in speaking of religious beliefs is a perfect example. The elusive connection between matters of faith and matters of fact has left a whole generation of analytic philosophers wondering whether religious claims really are the truth claims which they appear to be.

To find philosophers and theologians contending this question must come as a surprise to those who know little of academic philosophy. Religious assertions certainly *look* like truth claims; they take the form of indicative judgments, and we accept or reject them by saying that they are true or false. Moreover, we argue over these beliefs, defending them, doubting them, rationalizing them, and reinterpreting them in accordance with at least some idea of what a reasonable belief should be — all of which is characteristic of truth claims. Thus, with no reason to think otherwise, it must seem pointless to ask whether or not religious assertions are in fact *assertions*. The burden of proof rests with those who would deny it.

Yet there is a reason to deny it. The troublesome point is the "subjectivity" of religious claims, or the fact (so stressed by existentialists) that each of us has to decide such questions for himself. No one can answer religious questions for us, nor can we leave them for the "facts" to decide. The answers we need do not accumulate like the confirmed discoveries of public knowledge, and the absence of telling evidence forces us to take a religious stand without any objectively compelling ground underfoot. We know, however, that the truth or falsity of a *cognitively* significant assertion cannot be established simply by an act of choice, as if an ardent believer could turn his beliefs into truths simply by investing them with concern and commitment. A genuine truth claim depends on what is in fact the case, and to this extent its truth or falsity can never be settled by personal preference or arbitrary fiat. This dependency actually *defines* truth claims, so that any assertion which lacks this feature cannot possess any meaning as a claim to fact. Every so-called "subjective" claim, therefore, is bound to be suspect: if it cannot be left for the facts to decide, then it is hard to see how its truth or falsity could depend in any way on what is the case.

To make matters worse, the only clear cases in which we can show that our assertions depend on what is in fact the case seem to be *empirical* cases. If an assertion can be tested by empirical observations, then we can be sure that its truth or falsity is a function of the world, not of the believer. This was the idea which the logical positivists wished to capture in their "verification principle." What this principle is meant to say, in each of its various formulations, is that the truth or falsity of a cognitively significant assertion cannot depend on what is in fact the case unless it can be shown to depend on observable facts. On points of detail this principle has been hard to sustain; but ever since the positivists advanced the basic idea, philosophers have tended to think of empirical facts as the only facts worthy of the name and of empirical claims as the only factually significant claims.

Nowhere is this tendency more apparent than in the philosophy of religion, where the ideal of empirical testability continues to inspire noncognitivist accounts of religious belief. If religious claims go so far beyond empirical questions of fact that they are objectively irresolvable, then *knowing* can never take the place of *believing*. There can be nothing to "find out" if there is nothing to be actually, empirically, disclosed in

IV

matters of faith. Religious assertions, it seems, cannot be truth claims at all by this criterion. So unless one is willing to treat religious claims as empirical matters of fact, the only way to save the commonsensical idea that truth is at stake in religious belief is to break this lingering connection between cognitive significance and empirical testability.

1

Since empirical testability lies at the heart of the matter, it is crucially important to see why anyone could want to identify all questions of fact—i.e., all truth claims—with empirical questions. We have no *obvious* reason for thinking that every meaningful truth claim must be an empirical proposition. We know only that the truth or falsity of a proposition *must make a difference.* It need not make any emotional difference to us, of course, but it must make a difference in the world. The case in which a given proposition is true cannot be the same as the case in which it is false; otherwise, the proposition itself would neither *say* anything about the world nor depend on it. No meaningful distinctions can be drawn where there are no differences to mark out, and the distinction between the truth and falsity of an assertion is no exception. Apart from some corresponding difference in fact, this distinction simply cannot apply. So again, if a proposition is true, then something must be the case which would not be the case if it were false; if it is false, then something must not be the case which would be the case if it were true. One cannot get around this elementary point of logic without exchanging the concept of truth for some surrogate which has nothing to do with what is actually the case. Here, few if any would disagree with the positivists.

Few, however, would want to disagree; for if this is all that the definition of a truth claim comes to, then it loses its force. The logical requirement that the truth or falsity of a cognitively significant assertion correspond to a difference *in fact* is no less formal and no more cutting than the requirement that the truth or falsity of a proposition depends on what is the case. Difference in "fact," like differences in "what is the case," might cover anything from morals to mathematics. The mistaken notion that a reference to facts adds something here grows out of an ambiguity in the word "fact," which has a formal sense (1) in which any true proposition states a fact, and a material sense (2) in which facts make up the domain of empirical science. Yet the genuinely valid insight that the true/false distinction cannot apply apart from a potentially discernible difference in fact supports only the weaker formal requirement that the truth or falsity of an assertion correspond to a difference of fact in sense (1). This purely formal requirement says nothing about what a fact is, or how facts are to be ascertained—it says nothing, that is, about *empirical* facts. To arrive at some version of the verification principle, one has to conflate these two senses of the term "fact"; and to do that justifiably, one has to show that the purely logical concept of a fact in sense (1) actually entails the more restricted notion of a fact in sense (2). That takes another argument.

Interestingly enough, the logical positivists thought that they had found such an argument in Wittgenstein's early work, the *Tractatus Logico-Philosophicus*.[1] Since their approving attitude toward this book reflects a crucial gap in their own thinking, the argument of the *Tractatus* is worth looking into. Like the positivists, Wittgenstein denied the cognitive significance of every assertion which goes beyond "questions of fact"; but unlike the positivists, he continued to respect such faulty assertions (e.g., value judgments, religious beliefs, etc.) as expressions of deeply important human concerns.[2] Perhaps this disagreement amounted to nothing more than a difference in attitude, as many have supposed. Wittgenstein, however, also differed from the positivists in the way he drew the line between genuine propositions and pseudo-assertions, and this difference is more instructive.

Both Wittgenstein and the positivists attempted to establish some criterion for the identification of factually significant assertions, but Wittgenstein did so *without referring to any kind of verification, empirical or otherwise.* Instead of saying that a cognitively significant proposition must be empirically adjudicable in terms of observable facts, he said only that a proposition must have a *determinate* sense.[3] That to him was the essential point. A meaningful truth claim must say something about the world, something specific enough to enable us to tell just what would have to be the case for it to be true. Without this kind of determinateness, a proposition would leave its truth conditions too ill-defined to tell whether or not they are fulfilled. The difference between its truth and falsity would fade away in obscurity, and the very distinction would no longer apply. To qualify as a genuine truth claim, an assertion must be keyed to clearly specified — and thus potentially discernible — matters of fact. Otherwise it cannot possibly be given a truth value.

None of this should be very controversial. The idea that a proposition must have a determinate sense represents only one more variation on the theme that a *discernible* difference in fact must underlie the true/false distinction. In effect, Wittgenstein simply argued that differences in fact cannot be discernible unless they are clearly specified to begin with. Or to put it in another way, he stressed the importance of a proposition having a determinate sense because he realized that its true value must be *determinable* according to the way the world is. This sounds very convincing, yet it does little good in defining propositions unless we already know what it takes to give an assertion this kind of determinateness. Much of the *Tractatus*, therefore, is given over to the task of rendering the concept of a determinate proposition more perspicuous.

Again, however, Wittgenstein works toward this end without appealing to the notion of empirical verifiability. Instead, he develops the twin doctrines of "logical space" and the "picture theory" of meaning. Together the picture theory and the concept of logical space underwrite a "truth-functional" view of propositions. Ordinary propositions, in this view, are the logical products of "elementary propositions"; and the truth value of these elementary propositions determines the overall truth value of the complex propositions in which they come together as parts of a whole. Just as the values of the independent variables and constants determine the value of a dependent variable in a mathematical function, the truth values of elementary propositions and the "logical constants" which join them together determine the truth or falsity of the resultant complex propositions. Thus we can break down a compound proposition into a logically equivalent set of simpler propositions, and we can specify which of these simpler propositions must be true if the whole complex is to be true. That tells us the meaning of the complex proposition by telling us what must be the case for it to be true — i.e., by giving it truth conditions. Furthermore, by displaying these truth conditions, we can show that a (complex) proposition depends on a definite range of facts — those asserted by the elementary propositions which make it up. This presumably shows that it has a determinate sense.

Nevertheless, if this were all there is to the notion of determinate propositions, any assertion which could be reformulated as a product of simpler assertions would qualify as having a determinate sense. Such a requirement, in fact, would be practically vacuous, since it could be artificially satisfied by the conjunction of any two assertions, no matter how meaningless[4]. Obviously, a proposition could not have a determinate sense unless the elementary propositions which make it up were themselves determinate. But elementary propositions, by definition, are not *complex* (truth functional), and so we need some other explanation of how they acquire *their* determinate sense.

To give this second explanation, Wittgenstein turned to the picture theory of meaning and the doctrine of logical space. Propositions, he thought, could only acquire their sense by representing possible facts, but he knew that the idea of "representing a fact" and the idea of a "possible fact" were both obscure. Accordingly, he described logical space as a sort of structure in which all possible facts are given, and he explained the propositional representation of these possibilities as a matter of *depiction*. "Objects" of a meta-physically simple (unanalyzable) kind combine to form actual states of affairs, or facts, within logical space; elementary propositions picture these states of affairs by combining names for these simple objects in a parallel configuration. These objects, though, can only combine in certain configurations to produce facts, so the total number of possible facts is limited by the natures of these objects, whatever they happen to be. Such objects must not be confused with ordinary physical objects (which are analyzable and describable), nor should their interconnections be construed as spatial relations. They are really metaphysical fictions designed to convey Wittgenstein's intuitive sense of how propositions must relate to the world. He thought that propositions and the states of affairs which they represent must have some sort of common form, so he postulated irreducible names on the side of language and unanalyzable objects on the side of the world to make this idea of an isomorphic relation intelligible.

By producing a configuration of names, a proposition mirrors a possible configuration of objects in a logical space, rather like a schematic picture of chessmen depicts a possible position in the game. The schema is true only if that position actually obtains in the game at hand—i.e., only if the objects in logical space actually stand in this depicted configuration in the actual world. Hence an elementary proposition can be said to be determinate if it picks out *one* such possibility in logical space, just as a picture of chessmen can be meaningful if it depicts a unique position in a possible game of chess. Were a proposition ambiguous in this respect, we would not know just what possible state of affairs would have to hold to make it true; and that would mean that we could not give it a determinate sense by saying exactly what its truth or falsity depends on.

Anyone who has read the *Tractatus* knows that it is far more complicated than this sketch indicates, but since Wittgenstein adds nothing essentially new to this concept of determinateness, we need not go any further to make the relevant point. *Nothing in his theory of logical space or in the picture theory says that a proposition must be empirically adjudicable to be truth-functional, or to depict a possible fact.* Indeed, when one realizes that the facts in logical space can be identified only by the elementary propositions which depict them, one sees just how *formal* Wittgenstein's account really is. Suppose we say that "p" is a true elementary proposition; then the only way we can identify the fact which makes it true — i.e., p — is by using the proposition itself to refer to this fact. This tells us nothing, however, about the range of meaningful propositions that could be substituted for "p" here and therefore has no bearing on the question of whether or not there can be nonempirical truths. The question of whether or not there can be nonempirical facts, such as moral facts or religious facts, dissolves immediately into the question of whether or not there can be nonempirical truth claims. If there are, and some of these claims are true, *then they state nonempirical facts.*

Wittgenstein's early logical theory takes us no further than this. Hence the concept of a fact which emerges in the picture theory cannot be used substantively to define the range of all possible truth claims, as the positivists mistakenly supposed. To say that it belongs to the essence of a proposition to state a fact says only that "p" is a genuine truth claim if and only if it is true or false according to whether or not p is the case. While this is a true and proper thing to say, it does not justify the equation of cognitive significance with empirical content. That still requires another argument.

Now admittedly, when Wittgenstein wrote the *Tractatus*, he would not have agreed with those who say that there are all sorts of facts — moral, religious, metaphysical, and so on. If his logical theory had been that formal, neither he nor the positivists would have seen it as a sweeping condemnation of traditional metaphysics. Yet he did not draw his negative conclusions about the possibility of "higher" truths from the assumption that factual assertions had to be empirical; he drew them from the assumption that they had to represent *contingencies.* All sorts of nonempirical assertions "go beyond the facts" where the facts at issue are construed as contingent matters of what happens to be the case, as mere *givens.* Since Wittgenstein drew no distinction between facts in this latter sense and the facts required by his logical theory, he was able to define the limits of propositional language in a stunning way. Only contingent questions of natural fact could be possible truths. No "higher" insights, no moral evaluations or aesthetic judgments, no intimations of life's purpose — none of these things — could be cast into the form of cognitively significant assertions. Every attempted assertion about these things, precisely because it aims to express something which goes beyond a descriptive report of a contingent fact, leaves its truth conditions undetermined. Because there are no matters of fact (contingencies) to which the truth or falsity of such assertions can be reduced, they fall outside the limits of logical space, where there are no possible truths to be told. Inasmuch as religious assertions must reach beyond contingent matters of fact to incorporate these facts in a higher teleological perspective, they too must fall outside the bounds of propositional sense. Here the *Tractatus* leads to virtually the same conclusion supported by the verification principle: every transcendental, metaphysical, or supervenient claim must be a pseudo-assertion.

Notice, however, that the difference between Wittgenstein and the positivists emerges just at that point where each owes us a further argument. Wittgenstein thought that every truth claim must depict a contingent fact (since its truth or falsity has to be contingent on something), while the positivists assumed that every truth claim must state an empirical fact (since the difference between its truth and falsity must come out in some potentially discernible way). These two requirements are not the same. Take the assertion of the soul's immortality, for example. Insofar as the soul cannot be identified with anything observable like the body, the assertion of its existence or immortality cannot be empirically tested, a fact which led the positivists to treat the doctrine of personal immortality as a cognitively meaningless idea. Wittgenstein, though he came to much the same conclusion, arrived at it by following a different train of thought.

> Not only is there no guarantee of the temporal immortality of the human soul, that is to say of its eternal survival after death; but, in any case, this assumption completely fails to accomplish the purpose for which it has always been intended. Or is some riddle solved by my surviving for ever? Is not

this eternal life itself as much of a riddle as our present life? The solution of the riddle of life in space
and time lies *outside* space and time.

(It is certainly not the solution of any problems of
natural science that is required.)[5]

Presumably, the belief in the soul's immortality is one of
those "transcendental" beliefs which cannot be put into words.
Yet Wittgenstein seems to *accept* the possibility of the soul's
immortality in the course of his criticism. What, indeed,
prevents one from asserting the immortality of the soul?
Nothing — nothing, that is, except the necessity of having to
treat immortality as a natural, *contingent* fact, in which case
the "riddle of life" would remain unsolved. As far as logic goes,
however, one could still assert such a thing, and this claim
would be intelligible as a truth claim. It simply would lose its
religious significance.

Wittgenstein is obviously very cryptic about this, but I
think we can tell what he means. As an answer to the riddle of
life, the doctrine of the soul's immortality speaks to those who
cannot find any meaning or purpose in the brute fact of having
to live and die. In the face of such givens — these contingent
facts of life — the promise of immortality holds out a more
encompassing perspective, assuring us in effect that there is a
rhyme and reason to finite existence. To believe in it is to
believe that this life we now live is in some way a part of a
larger life in which the contingencies of our lives, the "riddles"
of fate, might be unravelled. It is to believe that the point of
our most purposive endeavors and the meaning of our lives is
not destroyed by finitude but somehow preserved against all
the twists and turns of fate. To underwrite these thoughts of
purpose, one need not have any *particular* conception of an
afterlife to propose; one only needs to accept the general
promise which this teaching represents — the promise of
something meaningful behind the apparent pointlessness of
finite existence. Yet this aspect of the doctrine, its very point,
disappears as soon as we present it as *one more given* or *one
more contingency* in human existence; for if immortality were

IV

something which we might discover as a brute fact of human life, then it would no longer convey any promise on the higher level where we question the meaning of all these givens. The riddle—i.e., the question of what to make of the given conditions under which we live—would remain. "Is not this eternal life [supposing that immortality is a contingent feature of human life] as much of a riddle as our present life?" Cannot the thought of having to live forever be just as spiritually disturbing as the thought of having to die? Yes, taken as *brute* fact, the immortality of the soul would promote the same kind of anxiety which the other contingencies of life already stir. And then it would fail "to accomplish the purposes for which it has always been intended."

Nevertheless, on the basis of Wittgenstein's logical theory one could still *assert* the soul's immortality as a natural fact. Whether or not this belief is empirically adjudicable does not matter; the only requirement is that the issue be presented as a question of contingent fact. It may be that every *natural* fact of this sort must also be empirically discoverable, but Wittgenstein never says this. As far as his logical theory goes, nothing precludes the possibility of nonempirical natural facts, or claims to fact.

As far as the *plausibility* of this theory goes, however, Wittgenstein's account sounds much better than it is. The doctrine of personal immortality, even as a "transcendental" claim, must carry *some* meaning; otherwise, Wittgenstein could never know "the purpose for which it has always been intended." If he did not realize the force of this assertion as a *teleological* claim, then he would not have seen that a naturalistic interpretation would destroy its point. Here Wittgenstein's logical theory fails to account for the meaning which *he himself* finds in "transcendental" propositions.

Wittgenstein may also have been confused on another point. The fact that the truth or falsity of an assertion always depends on what is the case does not mean that "what is the case" must be something contingent in the sense of being an uninterpreted natural fact. It is easy to become confused about this because we sometimes say that the truth or falsity of a proposition is *contingent* on reality, or that it is dependent on that which is *given* in reality. These expressions might make one think that every truth claim must be a claim about contingencies — i.e., raw facts *given prior to any kind of interpretation.* But to say that a truth claim is contingent on reality is just another way of saying that "p" cannot be true unless *p* is the case, which holds for every "p" *whether or not* it is a statement of natural fact. Consequently, if one says "the auto accident was bound to happen," the truth of this claim depends on the non-accidental character of the fact which it states — that the accident was *bound* to happen. This is not a "raw" question of whether or not the accident occurred, but a question of interpreting its occurrence in one way or another, as inevitable or avoidable. Of course, one might say that the accident was only bound to happen *given* certain prior conditions and natural laws, which are themselves contingent. (If we lived in some other possible world, these laws and conditions might not have obtained.) Yet if we can construe contingent claims this broadly, saying that some things are bound to happen given the world we live in, we might as well say that life has a purpose *given the world we live in.* Saying that such-and-such happens to be the case *given* this world is but another way of saying that the claim in question is not a necessary truth; it could be false. So *this* kind of contingency requirement, whereby the truth or falsity of an assertion simply depends on the world we live in, does not exclude those higher propositions which go beyond a mere description of natural fact.

Thus — and this is the only conclusion we have reached so far — we have yet to find any reason for invoking empirical or naturalistic restrictions in the definition of a truth claim. Both Wittgenstein and the logical positivists reached their conclusions about the cognitive insignificance of moral and religious assertions by grafting unwarranted assumptions onto the logical point that the truth or falsity of a proposition must depend on what is in fact the case. The positivists did this by confusing the epistemological concept of an empirical fact with the purely formal concept of an objective fact, while Wittgenstein did so by conflating the same purely formal concept with the notion of a value-free, uninterpreted given. In neither case did they justify these assumptions. Perhaps there are facts which cannot be empirically discerned; perhaps, too, there are facts about the meaning of our lives or about our moral obligations. Thus far, the burden of proof still rests with those who would deny it.

2

There is more to be said, however. We know that we can formulate grammatically correct but meaningless assertions, assertions which seem to make sense as truth claims but which actually do not. Some, such as "time repeats itself but never changes," plainly make no sense, while others, such as "a final purpose governs evolution," are less obviously nonsensical, if at all. Since the difference between sense and nonsense does not always emerge in the form of our assertions, and since we cannot always detect pseudo-assertions in our thinking, we need some methodical way of weeding out these meaningless propositions from our various areas of thought. Given only the requirement that the truth or falsity of a proposition depend on what is the case, we cannot establish such factual dependency if we can do no more than restate a proposition to show what difference its truth or falsity would make. If that would suffice, then we could confirm the propositional significance of "time repeats itself but never changes" merely by saying that its truth or falsity depends on whether time does indeed repeat itself. This simply begs the question, since all sorts of meaningless assertions might qualify as genuine truth claims on this basis.

In the verification principle, though, we have a criterion of cognitive significance which carries some force. We know that an assertion which is subject to empirical testing bears factual significance, because we can see that its truth or falsity makes a difference, a difference which we can discern in the evidence which we use as a measure of its truth. Thus we do not have to beg the question by defining the factual content of an empirical assertion "p" in terms of p itself. By citing the observable conditions which must be satisfied for it to be true, we can show that the distinction between the truth or falsity of an empirical hypothesis corresponds to a real difference in fact. This not only clarifies what it would mean for the proposition to be true; but, more importantly, it assures us that the true/false distinction rests on a discernible difference, a difference which we can tell.

When we turn to religious assertions, however, we find it much more difficult to correlate their truth or falsity with discernible differences in our experience. Consequently, we may begin to wonder whether or not the truth or falsity of a religious claim actually makes any difference—any difference in fact. Perhaps the world in which such claims are "true" is not discernibly different from the world in which they are "false." This is why Antony Flew's famous question—"What would have to occur or to have occurred to constitute a disproof of the love of, or the existence of God?"—weighs so heavily on those who want to defend their religious beliefs as full-blooded claims to fact.[6] To say that the factual content of "God loves us" comes out in the difference between the case in which he does love us and the case in which he does not obviously will not do for an answer here. If the believer cannot express the truth conditions of this claim in some other terms, so that we can see from some independent point of view what difference its truth or falsity would make, then we cannot be sure that its truth or falsity would make any difference at all. Yet if he can tie the truth value of his beliefs to the occurrence and nonoccurrence of possible events, then we can put aside this worry.

Still, why should the theist have to bring out the difference here in terms of *events*, as Flew insists? Why, in fact, must the true/false distinction rest on any kind of observable difference? The truth or falsity of a proposition must make a difference—this we all admit; and it must be possible to tell the difference—this too we can admit. None of this, however, means that the difference between the truth and falsity of an assertion must emerge in sense perception. "Telling" here can mean no more than "determining," since we can tell differences and apply distinctions in a variety of ways. Thus, one might argue more plausibly for a weakened criterion of cognitive significance by suggesting that the true/false distinction be restricted to propositions whose truth or falsity is, at least to some extent, *determinable*—i.e., determinable by any means. One might argue, for example, that the assertion "777 occurs in the expansion of π " actually has no sense as a truth claim because we have no mathematical means of adjudicating the matter. The difference between its truth and falsity may be one that no one could ever tell. Those who think that this mathematical assertion makes sense generally accept this criterion but insist that one could, in principle, resolve the question. Perhaps one could check a computer printout of the expansion of π, or perhaps one might be able to cite independent reasons for thinking that every mathematical proposition must be subject to demonstration. In any case, as long as it is logically possible to tell the difference between the truth and falsity of such an assertion, one can say that truth is at stake. One could even say that a mathematical *fact* awaits our discovery.

By this expanded criterion of factual significance, a proposition must be a *hypothesis* to be a truth claim; for that is just what a hypothesis is, an assertion whose truth or falsity can be independently assessed in terms of its truth conditions. Whenever one can say what would have to be the case for an assertion to be true—what data would have to be obtainable or what criteria would have to be satisfied, etc.,—then, instead of relying on intuitive judgments about its "correspondence with reality," one can handle the question of its truth indirectly by focusing on these conditions or criteria. As long as the fulfillment of these conditions and criteria can be determined in a way that does not presuppose the claim at issue, these conditions will provide an independent index of an assertion's truth value, making an *objective* judgment of its truth or falsity logically possible.

Yet an assertion need not be an *empirical* hypothesis to be objectively adjudicable in this sense. The truth or falsity of an assertion need not be tied to empirical conditions; any independent criterion of truth will do. The only important thing is that we have some independent index of truth so that we can recognize the difference between satisfying and not satisfying these truth conditions. That is all that we need to apply the true/false distinction in a meaningful way. Nonetheless, this amended version of the verification principle (with the empirical restriction removed) still cuts, since it excludes every putative assertion that has no independent truth conditions and that must be left to the believer's individual preference and fiat.

Arbitrariness, after all, is the one thing which must be ruled out if we are to make any sense of the idea that the truth of our assertions depends on what is the case. We commonly apply the true/false distinction wherever standards can be brought to bear on our judgments and wherever rationally *grounded* judgments are logically possible. Where nothing other than preference, or style, or conventional agreement governs our judgments, we no longer speak of truth. That is why it seems so natural to speak of the truth or falsity of mathematical propositions, and less natural to talk about the truth or falsity of various expressions of taste. In the mathematical instance we know that the acceptability of our assertions depends on certain conditions of derivability, which provide the means of distinguishing between those which are true and those which are false. In matters of taste we know that it is up to us to settle our own opinions. In the moral case we are not quite sure what to say because we are uncertain about the proper scope of personal choice in deciding ethical questions.[7]

Where, however, does this leave religious belief? If the "truth" of religious assertions can be decided arbitrarily by subjective decisions, then religious claims could not even pass this weakened criterion of factual significance. They could no more be *true* than any expression of personal taste, as their acceptability would not depend on anything other than the believer's own fiat. Thinking it so, in other words, would make it so—only this would not have anything to do with what is *actually* so in fact.

Consequently, it would seem that the whole long and drawn-out debate over the factual significance of religious assertions comes to rest on the question of whether or not religious beliefs can be adjudicated according to any independent criteria of judgment. Perhaps there are abstract criteria such as coherence or comprehensiveness in terms of which theological systems might be judged. Or perhaps there are experiences of a nonempirical sort in terms of which religious claims might be verified or falsified. More than a few philosophers have thought so; and if they are correct, meaningful religious assertions could be advanced, *as hypotheses*, on nonempirical grounds. Then one could speak intelligibly of "telling" the difference between the truth and falsity of such claims, which is all that logic requires of a significant, possibly true, belief.

Yet I do not think that we can leave it at this. There are undoubtedly some systems of thought that have their own internal principles of judgment and their own decision procedures, but have no dependent relation on the world around us. The judgments at which one arrives in such systems are simply acceptable moves in a propositional game, being no more descriptively appropriate to the actual world than to any other possible world. These judgments, though they may be acceptable (true) or unacceptable (false) according to the criteria given in the system, could not be true or false to what is the case if the system lacks any tie which ultimately binds it to reality. Astrology, for example, may be like this; if astrological forecasts and explanations are grounded solely in a given system of charts, so that their "truth" can be guaranteed irrespective of the world's course of events, then these forecasts and explanations could be true in *any* world—another way of saying that they could have nothing to do with the actual world. Indeed, this same worry applies to morals and mathematics, since one could argue that moral and mathematical systems of judgment are no more nor less appropriate in this world than in any other. The problem is equally severe for religious systems of thought.

In Christianity, for example, the acceptability of religious assertions is often determined (or said to be determined) by *authority*. If a teaching occurs in scripture or is endorsed by a church council or is uttered by the Pope *ex cathedra*, then it is supposed to be true. Yet it is difficult to see how the authoritative origins of a belief could guarantee its truth, since the truth or falsity of any cognitively significant belief must ultimately depend on what is the case, not on conventions and stipulations. No decisions, in other words, can turn a falsehood into a truth; therefore, the fact that believers can sometimes settle their doctrinal differences by allowing authorities to decide these questions does not show that the true/false distinction applies to matters of faith in the same way that it applies to matters of fact. It simply shows that there are certain norms which govern what an orthodox believer may and may not profess if he is to remain within the same community of faith.

Hence, it is easy to see why most theologians want to preserve a role for religious *experience* as an index of religious truth. The difference between a religious belief's truth and falsity must come out in some kind of possible experience, it seems; for there seems to be nowhere else to turn in defense of the idea that religious assertions depend on features of the real world, not on the needs and wishes of the believer. A tie to experience could establish the tie to reality which any cognitive system of judgment requires. It could establish a tie to reality, that is, unless the experience involved were so subjectively laden with interpretation that a person would already have to be religious to acknowledge its significance. That, however, is precisely what seems to be the case with religious belief. The appeal to experience, whether in defense of a single religious assertion or in defense of a whole order of religious judgment, invariably begs the larger question of faith by presenting the *telling* experiences in a religiously interpreted way. The believer experiences something which he describes as "God's love," or as "Jesus entering his heart," or (in the case of predestination) as "God's calling." The nonbeliever, on the other hand—who may be happy to admit that the believer has had some kind of experience—is hardly prepared to describe this experience in such a religiously presumptive way. To him it is obvious that the believer is interpreting his experience; and before he can take these appeals to experience seriously, he needs some assurance that the believer's interpretations are not gratuitously imposed on his experience.

Thus, it appears that we have come full circle, returning to the original issue of subjectivity without coming any closer to solving the problem. Given only the requirement that the truth or falsity of an assertion make a discernible difference in fact, we cannot *rule out* the logical possibility of making a factually significant religious claim (the concept of a fact and the notion of a discernible difference in fact are both too formal for that). Yet neither can we *rule in* this possibility. Religious claims may or may not be sufficiently independent of the believer to qualify as truth claims. So far we have seen only that the issue is more intractable than it seems.

3

To make any further headway at this point, we need to adopt a wider view of assertions; for the philosophical worry over the subjectivity of our judgments is not confined to religious beliefs. The same issue arises wherever we postulate indemonstrable principles to launch any kind of interpretive inquiry or to ground any kind of supervenient reflection. Wherever the judgments we make about the world go beyond a simple description of that which is immediately given to us in experience, one might wonder whether or not we impose our categories and concepts upon it. As long as one can distinguish between one level of judgment on which the facts are given and another level on which their interpretation is proposed, some such worry seems inevitable.

If, however, we had to exclude all judgments that go beyond uninterpreted statements of fact, relatively few assertions would pass muster as possible truths. Most of the knowledge we have accumulates on a level beyond that of rudimentary description, simply because we have to discipline our thinking to increase our understanding. We have to submit our experience to a variety of concepts and principles to make it intellectually and practically manageable. And we have to allow some place for these organizing principles in the logic of cognitive judgment; they cannot be dismissed as pseudo-assertions.

Indeed, we have to make a place for them as truth claims; for some principles are undoubtedly true. Take, for instance, the belief that the world has a past. Past events, simply because they are past, are never directly given to us in present experience; all our judgments about the past go beyond a simple description of immediate experience. Hence, when we explore the events of the past or try to explain their course of development, we assume that there is more to be known about the world than the direct description of present experience could ever tell us. We assume, in other words, *that there is a past*, and we treat the given facts of present experience accordingly. We construe various present experiences as memories, we describe various objects as remnants, artifacts, fossils, relics, records, and so. The knowledge of the past depends on this kind of interpretation and conceptualization.

Yet suppose someone demanded a warrant for the belief in the past and for the whole system of judgment that goes with it. Since judgments about the past go beyond the bare facts of present experience, how do we know that we are not imposing historical interpretations on the givens of our experience? Once this suspicion is raised, we cannot answer it very well by saying that our historical judgments can be checked against objective facts, because the relevant facts have to be historically understood before they count as evidence *of the past*. Thus, if the certainty that the world has a past had to stand the same challenge which Flew urged against the belief in God, it would not pass the test. "What would have to occur, or to have occurred," to disprove the claim that the world has a past? Presumably there must be some possible counter-evidence here if this belief is to qualify as a cognitively significant asssertion; but no past event could pose counter-evidence to this claim, nor can we imagine any future event which might weigh against it. The assumption that the world has a history is built into the very concept of an *event*. Events and occurrences, therefore, cannot possibly provide the *independent* grounds which the adjudication of this belief as a hypothesis would require. Nonetheless, we still think that the world does have a past and that this is a cognitively significant belief. So if anyone said that it did not make any difference *in fact* whether or not the world has a history, we could not agree; but neither could we show what difference the truth or falsity of this belief would make by laying out the evidentiary grounds on which it might be tested. The difference between its truth and falsity goes deeper than anything different bits of evidence could reveal. To pretend that the world had no past, we would have to transport ourselves beyond historical thinking altogether.

Similarly, if the principle that every natural event has a natural cause had to stand Flew's cognitivity test, it too would fail. What would have to occur or to have occurred to falsify this belief? An uncaused event? How could we ever know that an inexplicable event was uncaused? And how could we know that an event, which we think was caused, did not actually occur by chance? As long as we stick to that which is given on the most rudimentary level of description, avoiding any presumptive descriptions of events as caused or uncaused, the claim that every natural event has a natural cause will be logically compatible with any particular event which one could imagine. Yet this belief is far too significant to dismiss as a pseudo-assertion, subjectively imposed on experience. When we describe something as a natural event, we assume that it admits a causal explanation. We do not infer this from immediate experience, but neither do we read it into experience arbitrarily. To suppose that this principle is arbitrarily imposed on experience, one would have to give up the cognitivity of the whole order of causal explanation.

The resort to evidence in both these cases has a question-begging character, as it is bound to have whenever the principles at issue inform the description of the evidence used for or against them. If this question-begging use of evidence were rationally permissible, we could just as well answer Flew's original question about the belief in God by saying that the non-occurrence of various *acts of God* would count against the belief that God exists. If God had never created the world, never led the Hebrews out of Egypt, never sent his son into the world, never answered prayers, and so on, then believers would have no reason to think that he exists. The skeptic, of course, who is not prepared to describe anything as an act of God, will not accept an answer like that. All this "evidence" is saturated with a religious interpretation before it is ever presented, and so it does nothing to show that the believer's whole system of judgment, top to bottom, is not superimposed on the world of fact. Yet the logic of the matter in this case is no different from the logic of any supervenient order of judgment. Whenever the judgments we make involve any interpretation or explanation of the given—whenever they "go beyond the facts" in that sense—we can never test the underlying principles of our thinking without begging the question in the search for evidence. So we cannot reject the cognitive value of religious principles *on this ground* without denying the cognitive value of every fundamental principle of inquiry.

The lesson to be learned from all of this is disappointing but clear: to pin down the difference between cognitively significant beliefs (whose truth or falsity depends on "objective reality") and cognitively insignificant beliefs (whose "truth" or "falsity" depends on the believer), we have to look elsewhere. This, I admit, is not very much to offer by way of a conclusion, and I can understand why one might lose patience with these analytical difficulties when the credibility of religious beliefs hangs in the balance. If we pause to reflect a little more about the previous two examples, however, the one a virtual certainty and the other a reliable principle of science, we can still make a case for the cognitive significance of religious assertions.

One peculiar thing about believing in the past or believing in the uniformity of nature is that our believing shows up in our practice more than it does in our stated opinions. In the way we advance other beliefs or examine other opinions, in virtually everything we do in connection with our historical and scientific inquiries, we proceed without any doubt that the world has a past or that nature has an order which makes it

IV

causally explicable. That is why it sounds somewhat more appropriate to say simply that one believes *in the past* or *in natural causes*, for these beliefs come out in very general ways, too diffuse to be fully expressed in the claim *that* some particular historical or scientific fact obtains. Believing in the past is more like being "in" on the use of historical concepts. The agreement which is reflected in the use of these concepts can be re-expressed in the form of very general propositions which no one who shares these concepts would ordinarily think of doubting. That the world has a past, that events unfolding in the present leave others in the past, that every past event has successors which connect it with the present—all these things are taken for granted in the use of historical language. Similar assumptions could be drawn out of the common use of causal language in natural science. Here one believes by putting certain concepts to work, not by advancing any explicit opinions.

The belief *in God* is very much like this. The agreement of practice which is reflected in the use of theistic concepts can be expressed in the form of the working assumption *that* God exists, that he endowed the world with purpose, that he cares about his creatures, and so on. Among devout believers the agreement needed to endorse these beliefs is already present in their use of terms like "creation," "salvation," "providence," etc. Asserting these implicit beliefs, therefore, is unnecessary; they are accepted as soon as they are formulated. For those who are not religious, of course, all these working assumptions remain highly dubious. Yet the relationship here between employing certain concepts and holding certain beliefs is the same as it is in the nonreligious cases, despite the fact that the belief in God is (in our society at least) not so deeply ingrained nor as widely shared as the belief in the past or the belief in natural causes.

This connection between using a system of concepts and accepting a set of working assumptions makes it possible to recast the whole issue of cognitive significance in terms of concepts. Perhaps the working assumptions of a religious system of judgment are so readily acceptable to believers, and so unacceptable to nonbelievers, because these beliefs are part of a conceptual system in which they are true *by definition.* Instead of describing the world of fact, the fundamental tenets of a religion may describe only the conceptual scaffolding which believers bring to their experience. If that is the case, then these fundamental beliefs need not be any more dependent on fact than the definitions and working assumptions of an arbitrarily invented conceptual system. At least this way of putting the problem makes the difficulty a little clearer: to save the idea that truth is at stake in matters of faith, one needs to show what saves *any* conceptual system from the charge of being arbitrarily maintained.

To defend the cognitive value of a conceptual system one need not deny that the use of various concepts and the acceptance of certain beliefs go hand in hand. However, if this admission is supposed to show that every belief which is ingredient in the workings of a conceptual system must be regarded as a mere definition, devoid of any relation to the world, then one must object. The concepts and principles which we bring to experience make a difference in the understanding which we get out of it. The mastery of concepts is an essential condition for furthering our understanding; and to the extent that the mastery of concepts includes the acceptance of certain implicit beliefs, the acceptance or rejection of these beliefs can hardly be an arbitrary matter. They make a difference in what one can know. The difficulty is to explain how the difference which a whole conceptual system makes in our understanding can be told.

One way of doing this—a better way than the method proposed by Flew—is to imagine possible worlds in which our principles do and do not hold. This is not the same thing as trying to imagine falsifying evidence, since there might be worlds (including this world) in which our principles did not hold but could not be falsified. Admittedly, it takes a good imagination to invent these possible worlds. When we think of worlds other than our own, we usually make rather minor adjustments, substituting a few new facts for the given facts of this world. Changes like that, however, correspond only to the supposition that certain hypotheses which are confirmable in this world might not be confirmable in another world, where our *data* would be different. Thus, when we posit these other possible worlds and imaginatively travel between them, we unwittingly take with us the same *concepts and patterns of judgment* which govern our normal thinking. So the differences between these worlds do not go deep enough to touch those beliefs which are ingredient in our concepts, or in the *way* we think.

We might, for example, imagine all sorts of historical facts to be different in another world; but in inventing differences like this it would not even occur to us to alter the assumption that these facts can be temporally ordered, or that historical events develop out of previous events, or that remnants of the past show up in the present. We are much more likely to suppose that every possible world must be like our own in being subject to historical inquiry. Yet there might be worlds in which no change at all took place, or worlds in which all changes were so chaotic that events did not unfold or develop or leave any traces. If this is too taxing to imagine, consider the other example of believing in the causal explicability of nature. Here too we might imagine various natural laws to be different in other possible worlds, but that we could also imagine irregular worlds. In a completely chaotic world or in a completely changeless world the belief in nature's uniformity would not *suit* the facts. One could cling to it as a principle, but he would not get anywhere with scientific inquiry.

To explain the difference which the truth or falsity of a fundamental principle makes, therefore, one has to be more daring. Instead of playing minor variations on the particular facts which our systems of judgment have already turned up, we need to think of possible worlds in which these systems just would not apply — where our working assumptions would not *work* and our ideal forms of explanation would go unfulfilled. *This* world, after all, yields to our working assumptions about its past; the pervasive ordering of events in time, the search for new historical facts, the planning undertaken in view of the past, the sifting of memories, the collection of artifacts, and all

IV
___
117

the other activities into which the belief in the past is woven go on virtually without a hitch. We make mistakes in our historical judgments, of course; but historical thinking itself rarely runs up against any anomalies which stop it cold. That is why the belief in the world's past is more certain than the belief in nature's uniformity; the search for natural law explanations is sometimes frustrated by phenomena which resist this kind of explanation, such as parapsychological phenomena or subatomic events. Yet for the most part the world yields to this kind of accounting too so that the search for natural causes goes on in spite of these anomalies.

If we multiplied such anomalies on every side, we would find ourselves in a possible world where the belief in uniformity would be harder to sustain. It would not be falsifiable, but it would be less credible because we would have fewer successful natural law explanations to hold it in place as a reliable assumption. The same can be said of highly dubious principles and the actual world; the world does not cooperate equally well with every conceptual system. The astrological claim that every heavenly (astronomical) event portends an earthly one, for example, functions like a principle. It anchors a system of judgment which is based on a peculiar form of explanation, the search for portents. It says in effect that the world is *suited* to this form of explanation and to the forecasting which goes with it — only the system does not work very well. Not only is there no clear way to tell exactly *what* heavenly movements foretell, there is no clear way to connect specific heavenly events with specific earthly counterparts and thus no way to tell if particular events are indeed portended. The inability to make these connections, however, does not disprove their existence, and so the principle could still be maintained.

Having said that, though, we surely do not want to say that the actual world makes no difference to the credibility of such a claim. In the sense in which an assertion cannot be decisively falsified, and only in this sense, one could say that the belief in heavenly portents is compatible with any evidence which we might imagine. In the sense in which some claims are better suited than others to provide working assumptions for further

IV

inquiry, however, one could not say that this belief is compatible with all possible worlds. It just does not fit that well. It has to be forced over the facts, qualified by auxiliary hypotheses, and left hanging as an unfulfilled ideal. Other principles do not have to be maintained in this way; they fit more comfortably and leave fewer anomalies. And there is a "world" of difference between the two.

To draw all this together, therefore, one could say that there are *two* ways in which true beliefs might "correspond" with reality. They might fit the facts in the sense of being potentially verifiable by independently gathered evidence, in which case they would be *discernibly* true. Or, they might fit the facts in the sense of being suited to their intelligible ordering, in which case they would never be discernibly, demonstratively, true. The former truths describe the world's content, while the latter truths tell us about the general forms of understanding which this content allows. Principles are truth claims of this latter sort. They tell us that the conceptual systems which they underwrite — the "lenses" of which I spoke earlier — are *appropriate* to our experience, but they do not tell us exactly what is to be discovered in it.

If it still seems strange that there should be a difference between principles which fit the world and principles which do not, one more look at the practical side of the matter might help to secure the point. The understanding gained through reliable and appropriate (true) principles shows up in practice in the form of a *capacity;* and the failure to gain such understanding, due to unreliable and inappropriate (false) principles, shows up as a *lack of capacity.* Thus, in a world which does not bear his principles out, a believer must pay a price for holding them. Not only must he put up with more and more that he is unable to reduce to the form of explanation which his principles provide; he must do without those adjustments in his practice which a better understanding would bring. One can easily recognize these practical differences in the case of believing in nature's uniformity, since the mastery of this principle and the concepts which go with it leads to a greater ability to predict and to control natural events — something which is relatively absent in the life of primitive peoples who have no such belief. The capacitating effect of believing in the existence of the past is much harder to describe, but only because it is so pervasive. The patterns of judgment which depend on this belief enable us to adjust to the present, to see the events around us as the result of previous developments, to maintain a sense of continuity and identity, to accumulate knowledge, to anticipate the future—to do all sorts of things. These capacities are hard to describe because they are so manifold, and because we know of no people who have managed to live without at least some such capacities, dependent on some kind of historical thinking. It should not be necessary to belabor the point. Understanding the world around us is an achievement, and so it should not surprise us that the principles which promote or retard understanding should be capacitating or incapacitating. They are *supposed* to be capacitating.

There is no reason why religious principles should be any different in this respect. The belief in a Creator God is not so obviously capacitating as the belief in the past or the belief in natural law, but it belongs to the same general category. The kind of teleological judgment which it supports is supposed to provide a perspective in which the disturbing givens of human existence (the "riddle of life in space and time," as Wittgenstein put it) might be reduced to some order, and that in turn should help a person to order his values and his passions and to make some kind of practical sense out of his life. The insights to be gained by adhering to such a belief are not empirical discoveries of natural fact, nor do the capacities which the belief offers have anything to do with predicting or controlling the course of the world around us. If these insights exist, they are discoveries of purpose and intimations of life's redeeming worth. If they are genuine, they show themselves in "spiritual," inward capacities, such as the ability to consolidate one's selfhood, to resist despair, and to extend one's concerns to others. Many threatening anomalies—pointless events which seem to have no divine rationale—surround the belief in God on all sides. Yet the unprovable assumption that the life we are given admits a teleological rationale (which is what the belief in God entails) could be borne out by an increased capacity to reduce its riddles of purpose to a more intelligible order. By conforming one's thinking to the ideal assumption that there is a rhyme and reason to our existence, and by pursuing this sense of purpose along the lines suggested by auxiliary religious beliefs, a believer might discover a deeper self-understanding, a "calling," a sense of what life should be, a value in other creatures, or something else which helps him to interpret life's brute facts. Insofar as it makes sense to *wonder* about these things, it also makes sense to suppose, as a purely logical possibility, that there is a kind of understanding which answers to this wonder. And if the believer's capacity for resolving these perplexities is increased in accordance with the principles which inform his reflection, then it makes sense for him to claim some truth in his beliefs. If it does not, this need not be because his beliefs have no relation to what is the case. They could simply be false.

In sum, we now find ourselves more or less where we began — with a commonsensical notion of what a truth claim is. Wherever the distinction between the truth or falsity of an assertion rests on a difference which can be told, we can say that truth is at stake. This happens not only wherever we can tell the truth or falsity of a hypothesis according to evidence, but also wherever we can see our principles borne out in further discovery or frustrated by anomalies. These two types of telling, to be sure, are quite different; in the first the facts do the telling for us and a reasonable person must listen to what they say. In the second we must do the telling for ourselves, and others need not be compelled by the question-begging "discoveries" which we cite on behalf of our principles. Logic requires only that we avoid a totally vacuous distinction between the truth and falsity of an assertion, and this can be done without forcing every truth claim to pass muster as a testable hypothesis. We need only to show that purely subjective factors — fiats, preferences, wishes, arbitrary stipulations, and so on — do not govern the application of the true/false distinction. And when principles are at stake, these subjective factors do not — or at least need not — hold sway; for a principle must bear the weight of further inquiry, fostering some heuristic capacities, before one can believe with any confidence in its truth.

By this criterion those religious assertions which function as principles also qualify as truth claims. This does not mean that any of these beliefs are in fact true, nor does it mean that they would state the same kind of facts that empirical claims state if they were true. It means only that one cannot explain the substantial differences between religious assertions and other types of assertions by saying that some are truth claims and others are not. Instead, one has to trace these differences according to the particular concepts involved, the order of judgment in which they figure, and the capacities which they are supposed to promote.

Finally, we need not worry that this commodious account of truth claims, facts, and cognitive significance will countenance every syntactically correct assertion as a meaningful claim to fact. Some assertions are conceptually incoherent, and these lack cognitive significance because they lack intelligibility altogether. Other assertions are senseless because their affirmation or denial would not require any adjustment of *any* kind in our thinking, and these are cognitively insignificant simply because they are *pointless.* So we can still reject an assertion such as "time repeats itself but never changes," either because it is conceptually incoherent or because it is pointless. And we can still reject various religious assertions, if they too prove to be conceptually incoherent or pointless.

Logic, however, provides no justification for dismissing religious assertions *as a class.* To do that, one would have to show that teleological discoveries about the meaning or purpose of life never could arise in the course of a religiously disciplined way of thinking and living; and I am not sure how such a thing *could* be shown. Perhaps one might argue that no "discovery" of purpose deserves the name, but that would be hard to square with common sense. In the face of life's contingencies we feel the *need* for this kind of understanding, and we know that we cannot satisfy this need by arbitrarily inventing something to fill the bill.

NOTES

1. Ludwig Wittgenstein, *Tractatus Logico-Philosophicus* (London: Routledge and Kegan Paul Ltd., 1961).

2. There is ample evidence of this from several sources. Most of it is summarized in W. D. Hudson, *Wittgenstein and Religious Belief* (London: MacMillan, 1975), pp. 137f.

3. *Tractatus*, entry numbers 3.23, 3.25, 3.251, *passim*.

4. Any two propositions "p" and "q" could be conjoined as the single sentence "p and q," and the resultant complex proposition would then have p and q as its formal truth conditions — even if meaningless assertions were substituted for "p" and for "q."

5. *Tractatus*, entry number 6.4312.

6. Antony Flew and Alasdair MacIntyre, *New Essays in Philosophical Theology* (New York: MacMillan, 1955), pp. 96-99.

7. Interestingly enough, even A. J. Ayer found it necessary to argue against the logical possibility of rational moral arguments. Those who disagree in moral matters, he said, can only disagree significantly about empirical matters of fact, not about the proper assessment and evaluation of these facts. Their disagreement on questions of value cannot bear any meaning because it cannot be resolved; there is no way of telling who is right and who is wrong. Thus, he too implicitly accepted the idea that truth is at stake wherever our judgments can be submitted to independent means of judgment; otherwise, he need not have worried that someone might object to the verification principle by saying that we can submit nonempirical claims to impersonal standards of judgment. He wanted to deny that objection by saying we are *not* able to submit any nonempirical claims to rational adjudication, as if he would have to admit the existence of nonempirical truths if any were subject to such adjudication. See his *Language, Truth, and Logic* (New York: Dover, 1952), pp. 110-112.

V
THE PROBLEM OF JUSTIFICATION

Wittgenstein once said that he did philosophy "like an old woman who is always mislaying something and having to look for it: now her spectacles, now her keys" (*OC* 532). His problem was not so much that he set down his thoughts out of sequence, or that he was always running ahead of himself; nor was it simply that he had too many things to say all at once. Rather, he foresaw so many possible misunderstandings that he could not rest with just one formulation of any idea. Having tried to make his point in one way, he would restate it; then he would try again, and then, still fearful of being misunderstood, he would give up and start again with something which he had said before.

The problem which drove him to these stops and starts was the problem of explaining how some of our most rudimentary beliefs can be groundless without being irrational, and this same problem is bound to recur when the beliefs in question are principles. Principles can no more be derived from logically prior grounds than certainties; yet principles can be reasonably affirmed as *true* beliefs if they prove to be capacitating. That is the position to which we have come so far, but it is a point of view which is too easily misunderstood to state only once. It sounds too much like pragmatism, and the objections to pragmatism are too numerous to let the possibility of a reasonable faith rest on pragmatic forms of justification. The problem of justification is not that simple.

The capacities which one gains through the mastery of principles have *something* to do with their credibility; to deny that would be to overlook one of the few things that prevents the choice of principles from being arbitrary. It would be saying too much, however, to say that principles can be *justified* by their consequences, as if the beneficial effects of holding a principle could provide independent *grounds* for holding it. To take the practical effects of a principle as evidence for its truth or falsity would be to treat it as an assertion which is subject to a peculiar kind of testing. Practical criteria would replace direct evidence as an index of truth, but the underlying hope of adjudicating competing principles by independent criteria would remain. That would simply return us to the old assumption that every reasonable belief must be a hypothesis, well-grounded in evidence.

If that is where the discussion of principles and their capacitating effects leads us — away from untestable principles and back to hypotheses — then we too should stop and start again.

1

To see what we must avoid, we need only to look at the initially attractive but ultimately disappointing views of William James. He embraced a pragmatic theory of truth to bring science, religion, philosophy, and every other system of thought under the same canopy of rationality. Not surprisingly, he stretched a few points to do so; but his remarks are nonetheless engaging, and much of what he had to say is worth salvaging. In matters of faith, he wanted to defend our right to adopt "a believing attitude" without any logically compelling grounds to justify our commitments.[1] He was right to argue for that, but his pragmatic theory of truth was too crude to be convincing.

James did not invent pragmatism. The term "pragmatism" was actually introduced by C. S. Peirce, who used it to refer to a method of exposing purely verbal disputes. The gist of Peirce's thinking was that the thought of an object consists in nothing more than the effects which the existence or non-existence of that object might make on our experience. Thus, to clarify what it means to believe in the existence of a certain object, James paraphrased Peirce by saying, "we need only consider what conceivable effects of a practical kind the object may involve—what sensations we are to expect from it, and what reactions we must prepare," and so forth.[2] Once one understands these practical aspects of a belief, he knows all there is to know about the meaning of that belief. If he cannot explain what practical difference the existence or non-existence of something would make in our experience, then he cannot say that the assertion of its existence *has* any meaning.

There is a striking resemblance between this "pragmatic principle" of Peirce and the verification principle of the later positivists; but this should not surprise us, as both of these "isms" rest on the same point of logic. The pragmatic principle, like the verification principle, simply represents a reformulation and extension of the idea that all meaningful distinctions depend on discernible differences. On this point, James not only shares his deepest intuitions with the positivists but also draws a remarkably similar conclusion.

> Pragmatism . . . asks its usual question. "Grant an idea or belief to be true," it says, "what concrete difference will its being true make in any one's actual life? How will the truth be realized? What experiences will be different from those which would obtain if the belief were false? What, in short, is the truth's cash-value in experiential terms?"[3]

The moment pragmatism asks this question it sees the answer: "true ideas are those that we can assimilate, validate, corroborate and verify. False ideas are those that we can not."[4] Once the meaning of a truth claim has been tied to discernible differences in our experience, it is a small step to verificationism; and James, apparently, takes it.

However much he may have anticipated the logical positivists, though, James envisioned something other than a strictly *empirical* criterion of cognitive significance. True, he took verifiability as the definitive feature of truth claims, and he often spoke of pragmatic verification as something which reaches its terminus in sense experience; but he actually construed the notion of verification much more loosely than the positivists. How loosely he construed verification stands out in his treatment of particular cases. One finds the most telling example in his account of metaphysical claims, where he applies the pragmatic principle to one of the favorite whipping boys of the positivists, the Absolute of metaphysical idealism. On positivistic grounds, the belief that all finite distinctions are encompassed in an Absolute fails the test of cognitive significance, since the existence of this Absolute is compatible with any and all states of affairs. Nothing would be any different in our experience if there were not an Absolute. Not so for James; for him the existence or nonexistence of this Absolute makes a tremendous difference. Life itself, or the whole of one's experience, takes on a different character for those who share this belief. To believe in this Absolute is to believe that being itself ultimately absorbs and dissolves all finite evil, so that the evil around us no longer stands out *for the believer* as an absurd and debilitating fact of life. Each seemingly pointless evil loses its crushing effect in an aura of transcendental harmony; and to that extent, the belief in an Absolute proves its "value for concrete life" by restoring a flagging spirit and promoting a more positive attitude toward the inescapable conditions under which we live.[5]

So the existence or nonexistence of the Absolute *does* make a difference—only it is not as much a difference in sense experience as it is in the minds of believers. Thus, while believing or not believing undoubtedly changes the *believer*, the truth or falsity of this belief might not reflect any differences in the world of fact. James, however, seemed to think that the subjective importance of such a claim guaranteed its meaningfulness, as if the psychological importance attached to it proved that it was a meaningful *truth claim*. And that does not follow.

This apparent confusion over the concept of a meaningful truth claim is all the more surprising inasmuch as James praises the "pragmatic principle" as a means of detecting pseudo-assertions. He mentions, for example, a scientific dispute over the existence of "tautomerous bodies," a dispute whose details are unimportant except for the fact that it represents the sort of pseudoquestion whose purely verbal character can be exposed by examining its practical implications.[6] The existence or nonexistence of such tautomerous bodies would produce *no* effects in our experience and require *no* adjustments in our expectations, and therefore he rejects this issue as a meaningless dispute. Yet for the disputants themselves this issue might be invested with considerable emotional importance. Each party to the dispute might feel that he had much to lose, not only in terms of having one's judgment vindicated but also in terms of his sense of the fitness of things or harmony of the natural order. If so, this issue would take on the kind of emotional significance which James discerned in the dispute over the Absolute. That would make it a "meaningful" issue in one sense, but it would do nothing to show that it is anything other than a pseudoquestion of science. The truth or falsity of a genuine truth claim must correspond to an objective difference in what is the case, not to a subjective difference in those who invest their concerns in one side of the issue.

Again, however, James seemed to confuse the sense in which an assertion might be meaningful *to a believer* with the sense in which it might be meaningful *as a truth claim*. This confusion inevitably spilled over into his treatment of justification, and the result was a pragmatic view of truth-testing. For once the meaningfulness of beliefs was tied to the attitudes and expectations of believers, the reasonableness of a belief could be assessed in terms of the practical value of accepting or rejecting it. Once the point at issue in the dispute over the Absolute, for example, was presented in terms of the attitudes associated with belief and disbelief, James could say that the belief in an Absolute might be "validated" or "verified" to the extent that the attitude which it fosters enables believers to assimilate existentially perturbing experiences without becoming dispirited. Here the reasonableness or unreasonableness of a belief, like its meaningfulness, reveals itself *in the believer*. Once this point is passed, the rest is easy. Given such an expanded measure of truth, the concept of verification expands far beyond the boundaries of empirical science, opening up multiple domains of truth, each with its own practical standards of utility. Science offers us prediction and control of the natural world, or a kind of technological mastery; whereas religion offers us "serenity, moral poise, and happiness," a spiritual reward. In other domains of judgment other rewards apply; for as long as our beliefs make some difference in our behavior, we may expect some "characteristic kind of profit" to distinguish true beliefs from false beliefs.[7]

Even a sympathetic reader has to admit that James plays fast and loose with the concept of verification here. Yet most of the traditional criticism of his pragmatism does not go far enough to be very illuminating. Bertrand Russell, for example, claimed that the notion of pragmatic utility was too ambiguous to be workable. One could say that a belief in the infallibility of the Pope is useful (or useless) in all sorts of ways—as a means of social control, as a source of emotional relief, as a source of unity within the Church, and so on. Which standard of utility do we rely on? How do we know where the relevant consequences of such a belief end? And who is to say which of these consequences is really valuable? These sound like devastating questions, but James seems to have anticipated them. Evidently he envisioned a hierarchy of truth claims in which different standards of utility and therefore different types of verification would apply at different levels of judgment, all the way from the simplest kind of empirical descriptions to the most abstruse metaphysical speculations. The relevant kind of utility involved in the verification of these claims would depend on the *need* for judgments of any particular type. Thus, on the lowest level where empirical matters of fact are to be described, the truth of our assertions is to be determined according to their usefulness in helping us to anticipate and to organize our sense experience. On a higher level, let us say historical inquiry, the truth of our assertions would be judged according to their usefulness in helping us to expand a developmental perspective through which we understand and adjust to the present. Only as we move upward in this hierarchy would we come to religious and philosophical beliefs, whose vital personal benefits would serve as an index of their truth.[8] Assuming that a view like this could be successfully elaborated, Russell's criticism would dissolve, but other objections would remain. The difficulties with pragmatism go deeper than problems of ambiguity.

The simplest and strongest objection to pragmatic justification is to challenge the connection between utility and truth. Useful beliefs can be false. Pragmatists might argue that useful beliefs can only be falsified by *more useful* beliefs, so that the exposure of false hypotheses still depends on pragmatic considerations. But in the end this simple objection is telling, and it is telling for two reasons. For one, an assertion need not be a truth claim at all to serve a useful function. The belief in God, for example, might have no more cognitive significance than the belief in tautomerous bodies; and yet it still might promote "serenity and moral poise." One can grant such practical effects without thereby accepting the truth of this belief. The other reason for rejecting utility as a criterion of truth is that facts about a belief's practical effects are not the sort of facts which the satisfaction of its truth conditions requires. The facts which must obtain if a given proposition is true are facts about the world, not facts about the consequences of affirming the proposition. Thus, if pragmatic evidence consists solely of descriptions of a belief's practical effects, that evidence will never correspond to the facts which the belief's truth conditions entail. The only way to get verifying evidence out of a description of the consequences of holding a belief is to presume that these consequences would not have obtained *unless* the belief's truth conditions were fulfilled by the world of fact.

As an illustration of this last point, consider James's remarks about the practical verification of scientific theories. "Science," he says, "gives us telegraphy, electric lighting, and diagnosis, and succeeds in preventing and curing a certain amount of disease."[9] These technological achievements, attained in consequence of holding certain scientific beliefs, attest to the truth of those beliefs. They constitute pragmatic evidence in James's eye. We might very well agree in this case, but not because these accomplishments constitute logical grounds for belief in and of themselves—it is possible that light bulbs and telegraphs might have been produced by applying false theories. Rather we tend to accept the technological accomplishments of science as favorable evidence for the underlying theories because we are willing to grant the unstated assumption that such achievements *require a true understanding of nature*—i.e., that the practical achievements of science rarely if ever proceed from false hypotheses. Once we question that assumption, the technological accomplishments of science cease to carry any weight as compelling evidence for scientific hypotheses. Then the facts about various practical benefits derived from these beliefs no longer suffice as an index of their truth, and one has to look to evidence which has nothing to do with the practical effects of a belief to see if the given facts of nature satisfy its truth conditions.

The attempts to justify religious claims on pragmatic grounds represent a more obvious case of the same difficulty; for the assumption which we so often grant in the case of scientific beliefs—the assumption that the practical achievements of science depend on reliable theories—is a concession which we are reluctant to make in the case of religious beliefs. Instead, we are far more willing to assume that people can profit in emotionally satisfying ways from beliefs which are false. Psychologists and sociologists report all sorts of valuble functions performed by religious beliefs, and many of these beliefs are so patently superstitious that we have no tendency whatever to think that they are true. Some may say that these religious beliefs are "true" for those who hold them; but that simply reiterates the fact that believers receive some emotional benefits from their adherence to such beliefs. It certainly does not mean that these beliefs must be true in the strict sense of the word.

In any case, the practical consequences of holding a belief provide no real evidence of its truth unless we assume in advance that our beliefs cannot serve any useful function unless they are true. By themselves, the purely practical effects which attend the adoption of a belief do not prove anything. The facts needed to *ground* an assertion are those which correspond to its truth conditions, and these may be stated without any reference to the effects which the affirmation of the belief might or might not produce.

2

Appeals to utility, therefore, cannot save the reasonableness of ungrounded faith claims. The only question is whether some other form of practical justification might succeed where cruder varieties of pragmatism all fail. The capacitating effect of principles suggests as much, but it still is not clear how this aspect of principles can be tied to their justification without incurring the same objections which apply to traditional pragmatism. So perhaps we should stop and start again. Perhaps there is *another* version of "pragmatism" which suits the logic of principles.

Suppose, for example, that we restrict considerations of utility to those beliefs which we cannot possibly justify on any other grounds. The reason for such a restriction should be obvious; whenever we can adjudicate our beliefs on the objective grounds provided by factual evidence, we need not resort to pragmatic appeals. Rather than maintaining a belief for the sake of its practical effects, we can point to the relevant evidence and let it testify for us. That evidence might be difficult to obtain, and the little which is obtained might not reach very far; yet as long as an assertion admits the possibility of being grounded in this kind of evidence, we cannot afford to use pragmatic considerations as a reliable measure of its truth. In cases like that it is not only possible, but possible to show, that useful beliefs can be false. When the missing empirical evidence becomes available, it can testify *against* useful beliefs just as surely as it can testify *for* them. To avoid such conflicts pragmatic criteria should only be applied to beliefs which cannot possibly be verified or falsified on observational grounds. Then one need not worry that a pragmatically defended belief may later be shown, empirically, to be false. As long as such beliefs are truly indemonstrable, that could not happen.[10]

Yet there is no reason why the practical consequences of a belief should furnish telling evidence when the beliefs in question are indemonstrable claims, and unreliable evidence when the beliefs at stake are empirical hypotheses. If the practical consequences of a belief carry no logical force in the adjudication of hypotheses, it is hard to see how they could carry such force in the adjudication of principles. To suppose that the practical effects of adopting a belief have no role to play in the justification of one type of assertion, but do have a proper role in the defense of another type, one would have to acknowledge a fundamental difference between these two types of assertion. One type could be adequately judged in terms of its function according to pragmatic criteria, and the other type could only be judged in terms of its truth conditions according to factual data. The difference between these two types is so great, however, that pragmatically justifiable beliefs might as well be distinguished from the whole class of cognitively significant claims. What else could account for the peculiar appropriateness of pragmatic criteria in judging the one type of belief but not the other? The use of pragmatic criteria makes the most sense when the meaning of an assertion can be exhausted by a functional, noncognitive, analysis; for when the meaning of an assertion has nothing to do with the characterization of the world, there is no need to check it against the facts. As long as its meaning consists entirely of its relation to human behavior, it is ready-made for a pragmatic evaluation. Here the appeal to pragmatic criteria goes hand-in-glove with the noncognitive functions of various beliefs, so that the adequacy of pragmatic forms of justification depends on the lack of any cognitive significance in the beliefs at hand.

Thus, if one is willing to sacrifice the cognitive status of his beliefs, he can defend them pragmatically according to their utility. Wherever truth is at stake, though, as it is in most

V

134

matters of principle, this price is too high to pay.

The only hope of salvaging pragmatic forms of justification in connection with truth claims is to restrict the notion of utility to heuristic, cognitive value. This restriction has the virtue of restoring the weak link in pragmatism, the tie between what is useful to believe and what is the case. A heuristically valuable belief proves its utility by promoting understanding, either by facilitating the discovery of new facts or by encompassing known facts in a more illuminating perspective. This kind of utility is not an arbitrary feature of beliefs; it depends on how well the organizing role of a belief fits experience. Thus some regulative beliefs have more heuristic value than others, and, to the extent that this kind of value depends on the nature of the world, any belief which promises such value bears cognitive significance.

The trouble is that the heuristic or cognitive value of principles is hard to determine. How does one know when his principles have this kind of utility? And how can he convince others? The psychological benefits derived from certain beliefs, particularly from religious beliefs, do not guarantee its cognitive value; so how does the believer know that the "sense" which he discovers or the capacities which he develops represent *genuine* understanding? Philosophers of religion founder again and again on these questions, and with good reason. They have no simple answers. It is tempting to say that religious insights are intuitively clear of self-authenticating, and some theologians have even claimed that we have a special sense for religious truths. Others have said that such insights come by way of special revelatory experiences. To a skeptic, however, all such solutions sound like gratuitous devices for solving an unsolvable problem.

The problem *is* unsolvable if one expects a proof of particular religious insights, but there is no reason to deny the general possibility of increasing one's understanding through the adoption of religious principles. Just as we can tell that experience *eludes* our comprehension in some respect, however dimly defined this might be, we should be able to tell that we have *gained* some grasp of it, however provisional that might be. Here the "experience" which we need is not so much a sudden flash of insight as an accumulated ability to reduce perplexing aspects of life to some intelligible form of interpretation. That kind of experience is not peculiar to religious belief; we go through experiences like that time and again in acquiring concepts and mastering principles.

Think of how puzzling human behavior can be, for example. We explain it, assess it, and judge it in all sorts of ways; and we do this because it provokes reflection in so many ways. We are struck by what people do and want to know why they behave as they do, even before we know how to focus our interest in anticipation of any particular kind of explanation — a motive, a psychological cause, a reason, an excuse, etc. Moreover, even when we arrive at one form of explanation (a motive, for example), we may feel the need for another type of judgment (such as a moral assessment). That is why the principles and concepts which underlie our judgments of behavior "take" with us. We can recognize the *need* for further understanding; and having felt this need, we can appreciate the force of principles which provide the logical means — the discipline — to pursue it.

Or, to take another example, think of dreams. Here it is easier to imagine the inchoate curiosity of one who is haunted by dreams but simply does not know what to make of them. Such strange phenomena seem to have some kind of "meaning," but it is not at all clear what this meaning is supposed to be or how it is to be discovered. Psychologists hold forth a number of different principles, all designed to encompass the mysteries of our dream-life in an intelligible perspective. According to one view, dreams are sublimated expressions of repressed wishes; according to another, they are communications from an inner self; and so on. Each of these general statements about dreams grounds a corresponding pattern of dream-interpretation, and it is logically possible that one of these principles might enable us to discover the understanding which we seek in the "meaning" of our dreams. If so, this felt success is bound to reinforce the general perspective through which it was attained. Given the capacity to reduce opaque experiences to some form of understanding, the interpreter need not feel that he has imposed an alien, wholly gratuitous, system of judgment on his dreams. He may not know all there is to know about dreams, of course; but he might know enough to see that his principles promote *some* measure of understanding and, to that extent, bear *some* cognitive significance.

Similarly, those who feel that life in general, like a strange dream, must bear some teleological meaning might discover this meaning through the forms provided by religious principles. Of course, they may *not* find it either. Or they might deceive themselves by claiming discoveries which have no capacitating effect. All this is possible. Yet the fact that we can wonder about the terrible opacity of our fate also suggests that we might recognize its opposite, some higher purpose in life — if human existence has that kind of meaning. As far as logic goes, religious principles might be cognitively as well as emotionally capacitating. They might have their own kind of heuristic value, a value that we might miss without them and might appreciate through them. Duly revised, therefore, appeals to the cognitive utility of principles might constitute a fitting defense of their truth. Pragmatism of a sort might work after all.

Such an account is certainly richer than the usual appeals to experience; but in fairness to those who are skeptical about religious belief, it must be admitted that cognitively useful principles cannot be justified in any *strong* sense of the word. If one expects pragmatic appeals to furnish *objective grounds* on which to adjudicate principles, then no version of pragmatism will suffice. For even if various principles do lead to further understanding, and even if the believer is able to recognize and to appreciate this new-found understanding, the cognitive value of his principles cannot be translated into independent grounds for faith. The reason why heuristic appeals fail is the same one that spoils the attempt to justify principles on *any* evidential grounds: the insights and discoveries which bear out our principles lack the logical priority and the conceptual independence which rational grounds require. Since the believer's "findings" belong to the same order of judgment which his principles underwrite, he cannot possibly present them as evidence without begging the question of his principles' truth. He may *claim* to have discovered a higher purpose in life, or he may *claim* a greater capacity to make sense of his fate; but for one who suspects that the whole idea of higher callings and divine purposes is simply imposed on the world of fact, these claims will sound as hollow as the principles on which they rest. Maybe life has no higher purpose. Maybe there is nothing at all to discover in religious reflections. Such doubts undercut all *testimony* to the contrary.

Thus there is no *workable* standard of pragmatic value by which one might ground or test the truth or falsity of a founding principle of judgment, whether it is a religious principle or any other kind. Strictly speaking, one cannot even *test* a principle for himself, let alone justify it to the satisfaction of a skeptic. One has to judge his principles for himself in one sense, of course; he has to see for himself whether the kind of thinking which they support is in fact capacitating, whether it helps him to explain or to interpret his experience in any illuminating way, and so on. This, however, is not a matter of running an *experiment*, as if the temporary adoption of a principle was a means of generating *evidence* otherwise unavailable. The difficulty involved in the justification of a principle is not an epistemological problem of gathering evidence of any sort, either from within or from beyond the domain of faith. The difficulty is a purely logical one: fundamental principles undercut the priority of all evidence, no matter what kind it is or where it comes from. This is why religious belief, which is at bottom a matter of principles, never becomes *knowledge*. The believer who "leaps" into the domain of teleological judgment by adhering to some religious principles does not discover on the far side of the leap the compelling evidence he lacked on the near side. He may or may not acquire an increased capacity to make some sense out of life's brute facts; but his insights will remain so informed by the concepts and principles by which he took hold of his experience that they will never be translatable into independent arguments of belief, even for himself.

V

138

So if there is any sense in which an indemonstrable principle might be pragmatically justified, it is not the sense in which a justified belief is *well-grounded.* Logical grounds are provided by truths which we can accept *without having to accept the truths which they are meant to justify.* Neither religious principles nor any other fundamental principles permit such independence in their grounds, least of all in the grounds which are claimed for their heuristic value. This is just one more way of saying that principles are not hypotheses. We cannot test such claims by empirical means, nor can we test them by pragmatic criteria; for the evidence which we would offer in both cases is either irrelevant or overly presumptive. So if religious principles are credible at all, some other rationale must apply.

3

The problem of justifying religious belief cannot be solved by looking for any hitherto unnoticed way of grounding religious principles. Instead, the assumption that every reasonable claim must be grounded in prior evidence must be relaxed in favor of a broad view of rationality. Simple reflection tells us that some ungrounded beliefs must furnish the foundations on which we adjudicate other truth claims, and Wittgenstein reminds us how extensive this foundation of rudimentary beliefs is and how readily we describe these beliefs as "reasonable." Indeed, we think of the beliefs which are most deeply entrenched in our thinking, in the formulation of our doubts as well as in the defense of our opinions, as the most reasonable of all. Yet their reasonableness is not something they *derive from grounds.* They are reasonable simply because they play such a reliable role in our thinking that we have no reason to doubt them. Our thinking proceeds, our concepts develop, and our knowledge accumulates; and the weight of all this on-going inquiry presses these rudimentary beliefs beneath the threshold of sensible questioning, shifting the burden of giving grounds from the side of belief to the side of doubt.

Could not the same sense of "reasonableness" also apply to principles? Logically, there is no reason why the demand for logical grounds might not subside for one who doubts certain fundamental principles just as it does for the child who is told to accept various unquestionable certainties. Being capacitated by these principles, a believer may find the thinking which follows from them "weighty" enough to hold them in place, thereby shifting the burden of argument from the side of conviction to the side of doubt. One who masters a principle and finds it capacitating gains the benefit of the doubt, so to speak. He does not come into possession of any unambiguous insights that he might turn into logical grounds for belief, either for himself or for a skeptic. Yet he might well overcome the *need* for such grounds. As the axis of his faith is steadied by the judgments which surround it, the unfulfilled and unfulfillable demand for rational grounds becomes less damaging to the credibility of his principles. As long as he gains some conceptual hold on his experience through these principles, he can ignore the demand to justify them on prior grounds; and as long as no specific reasons for doubt renew this demand, he cannot be accused of irrationality.

If this way of extending reasonable beliefs to cover indemonstrable principles seems artificial, one should remember that principles (unlike certainties) are subject to *groundless* doubts. They institute supervenient levels of judgment which cannot possibly be justified on the levels which they are meant to supplant. Judgments of (contingent) fact never add up to judgments of value, and moral assertions never quite add up to religious claims. Moral judgments encompass what *is* with judgments of what *ought to be,* and religious reflection incorporates both of these forms of judgment in a higher level of reflection aimed at the *raison d'être* of all that is and the *point* of striving for what ought to be. Thus, from the point of view of one whose reasoning moves only along one of these lower levels of judgment, the higher level may seem suspect for no other reason than the fact that judgments on this level differ too much from his familiar thinking to "make sense." Wherever alien principles are advanced to raise the would-be believer's thinking to new levels of discernment, such doubts are sure to arise. These doubts require no special arguments to back them up, but they do require a response.

Without some way of removing groundless doubts about principles, there is no way to avoid a host of pernicious "isms" — fideism, relativism, fanaticism, dogmatism, and so on. Yet — and this is the crucial point — the possibility of overcoming these groundless doubts need not depend on only one model of reasonable belief. Every reasonable belief needs to be protected from doubts, but every doubt does not have to be washed away by argument. The groundless doubts which people have about indemonstrable principles are generalized doubts which apply throughout whole systems of judgment, and the only way of overcoming them is through an equally general appreciation for the systems themselves. In the face of such doubts no one judgment within a system is any less suspect than another, and none, therefore, can be defended in isolation. Rather, the system as a whole needs to be defended; but that cannot be done by "grounding" its principles in some other system. To resolve one's doubts about fundamental principles, one needs to see what is to be gained through the kind of reflection they institute. One needs to see the difference, that is, between accepting our experience as is, according to familiar forms of description, and bringing it under a new rubric of interpretation. Such "seeing" does not supply an objective criterion for selecting principles, since the insights involved cannot be independently described and set forth. A working knowledge of principles never supplies the sort of data which can be turned into independent grounds for belief. Yet it can transform one's groundless doubts about the cognitive value of certain principles into a weighty appreciation for them. That, in the absence of any further reasons for doubt, is all that a reasonable adherence to principles requires.

This last point is the crucial one. No appeal to the usefulness of a principle, whether it is an appeal to its psychological value or to its heuristic value, will ever satisfy the demand for rational justification as long as the only "justified" beliefs worthy of the name are warranted inferences from logically prior grounds. By that standard of rational justification religious principles cannot qualify as reasonable beliefs, but neither can any other principles. Principles can be reasonably held only in the sense that they can be *appropriately* or *unobjectionably* maintained. Any belief can be reasonably maintained in this relaxed sense if one has no reason *not* to hold it—i.e., if one has no ungrounded doubts about its cognitive value and every specific objection to it can be met. In the case of principles, this first condition can be satisfied (in theory) through the acquisition of those conceptual capacities and interpretive abilities which their mastery is supposed to provide. Then, as long as there are no other objections to be faced, the believer gains the benefit of the doubt. The burden of argument shifts to the side of the skeptic, who cannot begrudge the appropriateness of the believer's convictions without giving his *own* reasons.

The groundless doubts of the skeptic, in other words, do not give him the logical right to gainsay the believer's confidence in his principles. The believer cannot prove that his insights are genuine. He cannot prove that his ability to discover more sense is anything more than a psychological benefit which he has gained through his convictions. Yet he does not have to prove these things; to expect that is to expect too much. Principles, in this respect, are much like certainties: certainties are so deeply ingrained in every thought and practice that one who would doubt them owes us an argument against them. Principles are not so deeply ingrained in our thinking; but once inquiry has begun to flourish on the foundation which a set of principles provides, reason no longer requires an objective certification of their cognitive value. The believer who feels that his principles give him a better hold on his experience has all that he needs to answer his groundless doubts about their value, and his sense of increased understanding gives him the *prima facie* right to his convictions. It is possible, of course, that the believer's "insights" are read into his experience for psychological reasons; but the mere possibility that this might happen is not enough to accuse the believer of irrationality.

V
142

The general possibility of confusing the psychological value of various regulative beliefs with their cognitive value no more justifies the charge of irrationality in matters of principles than the abstract possibility of error justifies philosophical skepticism in matters of certainty. In both cases believers are entitled to their convictions *until* skeptics can produce articulate objections against them.

This account of reasonable belief is not an invitation to fideism or fanaticism. The capacities which one acquires through the mastery of principles protects these principles only from those unfocused doubts that are the product of unfamiliarity and the lack of appreciation for the kind of judgments at issue. If there are other doubts — grounded objections — to be considered, then these objections must be answered, and answered in kind with specific arguments. As an answer to all forms of doubts and every objection to indemonstrable principles, the believer's working confidence in his convictions will not suffice. The benefit of the doubt does not extend *that* far; it only excuses the believer from the unfulfillable demand to prove that his principled way of thinking leads to *real* understanding. Beyond that every other reason for doubt returns the burden of argument to the believer.

Those who accept the belief in nature's uniformity, for example, can be said to hold a reasonable conviction, not because they have any independent evidence for this ungrounded belief but because the success of scientific inquiry reduces the *demand* for justification by answering the believer's doubts about its value in promoting further understanding. There is no way that scientific believers can translate this increased understanding into an independent argument for believing in uniformity, but they do not have to: it is still a reasonable belief. Yet if prescientific peoples should produce articulate objections against this belief — objections based on independent rational criteria — then this would renew the demand for justification. The believer would then owe the skeptic reasons for belief — but these reasons would still not entail the derivation of the belief in uniformity from independent grounds.

"Justifying" the belief would simply be a matter of answering every grounded objection to it.

The justification of religious principles is essentially no different. The believer who feels capacitated by his beliefs owes the skeptic reasons for belief, but only reasons in answer to specific reasons for doubt. The reason that religious principles seem to require a stronger form of justification is that specific reasons for doubt are so readily available. Religious claims often seem to conflict, either with themselves or with well-established scientific and historical claims. Sometimes they offer cumbersome explanations of phenomena which can be explained in simpler ways. Sometimes they seem conceptually incoherent. A reason for suspecting any of these possibilities is reason enough for doubt, and wherever such doubts exist they need to be answered. Yet they need to be answered *one by one*, for there is no way that the truth of religious principles can be independently established in advance of all objections. Even when the air is full of reasonable suspicions and some defense of a principle is badly needed, a truly fundamental principle can never be justified as an inference from prior, more certain grounds. The only defense of such principles is a counter-argument against the reasoned grounds for unbelief, so that the capacitating effect of a principle can be left to believers and potential believers to judge for themselves.

The justification of traditional theism, for example, often becomes so bound up with the solution of the problem of evil that the two become indistinguishable. Since this problem is a problem of reconciling three seemingly inconsistent doctrines, it can be solved by removing any reason to suppose that these three claims (about the omnipotence of God, the perfect goodness of God, and the existence of evil in God's creation) are mutually inconsistent. One can call this a "justification" of theism if he likes, as it does represent a *defense*. Yet it secures the beliefs at issue only against one reason for doubt, leaving the larger question of faith where it stood before. Or to put it another way, a solution to the problem of evil (if there is one) would show only that a reasonable commitment to traditional theism, in the absence of other reasons for doubt, is a logical possibility. Such a possibility must be established against all objections, but reasoned responses to these objections should not be confused with positive grounds for belief.

Even so, the fact that such responses to particular objections often *pass* for "justification" is revealing. It shows that the benefit of the doubt *does* rest with the believer who, on the one hand, finds his beliefs to be capacitating and, on the other hand, is able to meet every specific charge made against them. If that is how it is, then the believer is entitled to his convictions — logically entitled — even though he cannot ground them in prior evidence or derive them from prior premises.

It is hard to see how truly fundamental principles could be held in any other way. In the end, when every grounded doubt has been answered and only an uneasy suspicion remains, the confidence that comes and goes by relying on a principle is the only appropriate measure of its truth. There is nothing unreasonable about that. Every kind of justification must come to an end eventually in the tacit assurance that the principles by which we think and live are suited to our experience and can be borne out in the actual practice of trying to understand the world around us.

No doubt the many alternatives held out to us as fundamental religious principles may make us wish for stronger forms of justification. We would like to justify one religious alternative exclusively and in advance of all the others; failing that, we would rather avoid exclusive commitments by telling ourselves that all religions are essentially compatible. Yet the logic of religious principles does not admit such easy solutions. Because truth claims are at stake, there is a special uncertainty in having to adopt and sustain one set of principles in the midst of so many secular and religious alternatives. We are not sure whether or where to leap, or what to say about the alternatives we leave behind. This difficulty, however, looks worse than it is. Ungrounded religious convictions need not be blind or presumptuous, and we need not abandon the logic of principles to see why. We simply need to carry the account one step further.

NOTES

1. William James, *The Will to Believe* (New York: Longmans, Green, and Co., 1898), pp. 1-2.

2. William James, "What Pragmatism Means," in *Pragmatism* (New York: Longmans, Green, and Co., 1907), pp. 46-47.

3. From "Pragmatism's Conception of Truth," *Pragmatism*, p. 200.

4. *Ibid.*, p. 201.

5. From "What Pragmatism Means," *Pragmatism*, pp. 73-74.

6. *Ibid.*, pp. 48-49.

7. William James, *The Varieties of Religious Experience* (New York: Longmans, Green, and Co., 1902), pp. 122-123.

8. See Lecture XVIII, *Varieties*, pp. 430-457.

9. *Varieties*, p. 122.

10. James apparently had such a restriction in mind when he spoke of "over-beliefs" — i.e., beliefs which overreach the evidence available for them. Yet the evidence which over-beliefs exceed was itself pragmatic, so that the judgment of over-beliefs involves the exchange of one standard of utility for another, higher, standard.

VI
THE EXCLUSIVENESS OF
RELIGIOUS CONVICTION

According to his biographer, Spinoza's landlady once asked him if he thought that she could be saved in the religion she professed, and Spinoza gave her the following gently moving answer: "Your religion is a very good one; you need not look for another, nor doubt that you may be saved in it, provided, whilst you apply yourself to piety, you live at the same time a peaceable and quiet life."[1] The woman was probably a Christian of some kind, but it makes little difference, as Spinoza regarded any religion which promotes a virtuous life a "very good one" in which a devout person may be "saved." The point of believing is not to possess more knowledge but to live more truly, for the saving blessings of religion attend the quality of one's life and not the correctness of one's opinions. *True* faith is not a matter of knowledge at all, but of obedience; and so the simple believer who bends his will to the demands of right living, while applying himself to piety, stands fast in God's truth no matter what his beliefs may be.[2]

This easy acceptance of other religions made Spinoza a radical and dangerous thinker in his day. In our day a similar perspective has become almost a requirement of philosophical analysis, as if any *other* account would summon forth all the horrors of militant, dogmatic religion. All but the most conservative theologians have thrown away the old assumption that only one religion can be true, lest their indemonstrable affirmations be presumptuously converted into denials of another person's faith. To avoid this problem some people would rather avoid religious controversies altogether. Others, who are more sympathetic to religion, would rather make their affirmations so broad that no one's religious views are implicitly denied. That way, if there is any truth or happiness to be found in religion, one can cast a net widely enough to cover it.

The only trouble with this last approach is that it is hard to make any inclusive affirmations of faith without also making some denials. The traditional way of attempting this trick is to draw a distinction between the essential and the inessential content of religion, making sure to construe the essence of true religion broadly enough to include every religion about which anyone is likely to care. Then the points of disagreement where religious conflict seems unavoidable can be treated as inessential aspects of religious belief, which no one is under any obligation to defend. The other way of avoiding exclusivity in judgments of faith is Spinoza's way. One adopts a non-cognitive approach, denying that truth and knowledge are at issue in religious belief and suggesting that religious teachings acquire their value by serving some other function. This allows apparently contradictory beliefs to be given the same positive evaluation, not as truth claims but as linguistic devices for achieving some other end. Spinoza was one of the first to try this strategem, but he has had many successors. He judged religious beliefs in terms of their practical value in promoting a virtuous life, whereas his successors have evaluated them largely in terms of their psychological or sociological value. The general result is the same: a belief may be functional for one person and disfunctional for another. Or two apparently irreconcilable beliefs (e.g., the belief in personal immortality and the belief in individual extinction) may both perform valuable functions in their separate settings. In no case does the affirmation of one belief's functional value entail a denial of the value of any other belief. That kind of inference is cut off by noncognitive accounts. Indeed, once the ordinary logic of assertions dissolves in this way, the apparent exclusivity of religious belief also disappears, and a pluralistic affirmation of different religions becomes not only a possibility but a virtual necessity.

There are very strong commonsensical reasons, however, for not adopting any completely noncognitive approach to religious belief; the functions and practical consequences of religious beliefs are normally part and parcel of the belief that certain things are *true*. Faith, as the believer understands it, must be grounded in something other than the needs which it serves; otherwise it would not make sense for the believer to doubt his beliefs, to worry that he might be living an illusion, to heed his critics, or to defend the consistency of what he believes. In fact, if one were to affirm only the function of a belief, and not the belief itself, as a truth claim, the belief would *cease* to function in the way it does for ordinary believers. One who doubts this point need only consider, for example, the difference between believing that the resurrection of Jesus actually took place and believing that the thought of his resurrection serves a useful function. Ironically, the second belief completely *lacks* the reassuring psychological and moral affect which is supposed to justify the first. This second belief, in other words, is a different *belief* altogether, not a different (nonexclusive) way of affirming the first — all of which shows that purely functional affirmations of religious assertions violate their logic.

Spinoza, interestingly enough, knew better than that. Instead of maintaining a completely noncognitive approach to religious belief, he laid down seven "dogmas of universal faith," stating plainly that anyone who does not hold these *truths* cannot partake of the true faith.[3] Thus, he combined a noncognitivist's approach with an essentialist's strategy, treating the essential doctrines of true religion as genuine assertions and confining his noncognitive appraisals to inessential doctrines. To ground his own religious pluralism, he advanced the sort of claims which dictate a life of obedience and virtue — if they are true. On this point he was not so tolerant of other views. Only some beliefs were optional; the seven dogmas were absolute requirements of true faith.

Inevitably, therefore, Spinoza retained some exclusive religious views. As soon as he set forth his universal dogmas of true faith, he committed himself to denying all contrary beliefs. Those who disagree with the seven dogmas he could not have accepted as true believers. Their lives, of course, he might have affirmed, but their incompatible beliefs he could not have endorsed. Consequently, he condemned exclusivity in religion without altogether escaping it, and those who have followed him in trying to disentangle the essential content of true religion have invariably done the same. One cannot possibly define the essence of true faith in propositional terms without committing oneself to an implicitly exclusive position. Yet one cannot do justice to religious belief by entirely severing it from propositions, either. If we are to find some basis in logic for the unassuming faith which we admire in practice, therefore, we will have to discover a third alternative.

1

I see no escape from denying the truth of every belief which is incompatible with one's own beliefs. To give up this kind of exclusiveness would be to sacrifice one's beliefs as truth claims. Yet this does not mean that we have to develop our religious convictions by passing judgment on every alternative. In matters of faith there is a certain asymmetry which leaves one in a better position to affirm one's own beliefs than to deny those of another. Every believer must in his own mind reject incompatible doctrines, but it is not always possible to tell how compatible or incompatible other religious beliefs are with one's own. Nor is it necessary to decide these questions in order to develop one's belief in a reasonable way. The alien beliefs of other religious cultures do not have to be affirmed or denied; often they can simply be ignored.

The peculiar asymmetry of religious judgment, and the benign neglect which goes with it, result from the fact that principles are at stake in matters of faith. The affirmation of principles depends on certain conditions which are not always filled as the believer turns his attention from one set of religious claims to another. Before he can adopt them, the believer must understand the point which these beliefs acquire as regulative claims; and before he can resolve his doubts about them, he must appreciate their force in framing a new dimension of reflection. Yet a potential believer generally has this kind of familiarity with only a few religious traditions, sometimes only one. Thus he can deal responsibly only with those for which he has a working understanding. The others he must ignore until he is in a position to evaluate.

To show how different this is from an easy relativism or a harsh dogmatism, Spinoza's reply to his landlady can be compared with a story from Kierkegaard. In a passage in his *Journals*, Kierkegaard considers the objections which a Christian's commitment to only one means of salvation is likely to provoke. To one who has found new happiness in Christ, he says, "the only possible objection would be: but you might possibly have been saved in another way." Yet to this objection there is no answer. "It is as though one were to say to someone in love, yes, but you might have fallen in love with another girl; to which he would have to answer: there is no answer to that, for I only know that she is my love."[4] Kierkegaard thought that this is how it is for the devout believer, too. Inasmuch as the believer has found through faith the understanding which he seeks—and inasmuch as he has no *other* reason to doubt the teachings which have brought him to this understanding—he need not know or care whether he might have made sense of his life in some other way.

This analogy between faith and love is not perfect (why should it be if it is only an analogy?), but one can press it a long way before having to give it up. One who is in love need not pass judgment on every other person whom he might have loved, not because finding a mate is such a relative thing that anyone will do, but because finding a mate is not something one can do in the abstract. It takes a certain amount of intimacy, a working personal relationship, to know that one's choice of another could not have blossomed into a happy love. We just do not have that kind of relationship with very many people. Some would-be mates, I suppose, can be ruled out without entering into any special relationship with them. Perhaps they are too old or too young, too morally offensive or culturally different. Nevertheless, the fact that we can exclude some people for reasons like this does not mean that we can find the persons we seek simply by narrowing the options. There will always be other people of whom we could not say — without being presumptuous — "I could never possibly love her (him)." One just does not know whether love might or might not grow without giving it a chance. One thing we do know, however, is that love is not self-assuring. We can make mistakes in such matters, devoting ourselves to relationships which are never happy and which can never truly flourish, so there is good reason to be anxious in choosing one's beloved. Love must be ventured, and those who venture their love can be expected to have some doubts and to *need* some assurances.

In fact, one could imagine a certain type of philosopher becoming quite distraught about this. Given so many alternatives and so much at stake, he might demand further criteria by which to make a choice. Any other way of proceeding, he might say, would be arbitrary, irrational, and unsafe. Indeed, we can easily imagine someone who, in the name of rationality, tries to set up a fully determinative list of criteria for choosing a mate, so that the risk of making a mistake might be eliminated. Perhaps he draws up a list of ideal characteristics and then proceeds to measure every potential selection against this ideal. Perhaps he even claims that this is the only *reasonable* way to seek a suitable mate. Far from being reasonable, however, this approach to love is actually comical. Our would-be lover sets out to choose his beloved in such a way that the correctness of his choice might be objectively established, thinking that this will save him the trouble and the risk of making any subjective judgments. Thus he chooses his mate as one would choose, say, an automobile — strictly impersonally, strictly rationally. We laugh at this because it is so ironic; he wants to be reasonable, but he winds up acting like a fool.

The reason why such an impersonal approach is foolish is that objective criteria are not *unconditionally* telling. One might reject a potential mate for being too unattractive, for example, whereas the same person might become very attractive if one only knew her (him) better. Here the judgments which one makes are conditioned by the quality of the relationship which underlies them. If one's relationship to another is mutually sustaining and enriching, so that the love which is given and returned consolidates itself, then all those things which otherwise would count as objections against the beloved are reduced in their importance or eliminated altogether. The unattractiveness which others see in the beloved becomes, for the lover, attractiveness; the irritating habits become endearing idiosyncracies; the socially offensive behavior becomes a mark of integrity, and so on. These appraisals are obviously biased in one sense; the lover who makes them stands in a very special relationship with the person being judged. But can we blame him (her) for this? Is it unreasonable for the lover to allow this personal relationship to affect his (her) thinking about the beloved? Or should the lover only use the kind of impersonal judgment by which the beloved might be compared with all other possible mates?

The answer is clear. The only reasonable way to find a suitable mate is to become appropriately "biased" in a personal relationship. Prior to establishing such a relationship, one might well seek someone who is attractive or engaging in some other way; but this sort of judgment, which applies in *surveying* the field, must eventually give way to another kind of test. One ventures his own love in the hope that it will be requited and augmented. There is no other way to resolve one's doubts about choosing one mate out of a multitude of possibilities. Here one's choice need not be grounded so much as sustained, for a love that sustains itself needs no further justification. The doubt that once existed in the face of alternatives simply disappears in a happy love.

The lover whose love is vindicated in this way possesses no criteria by which to justify his love vis-a-vis every possible alternative, but neither does he need such criteria. Indeed, if he should sing the praises of his beloved too loudly, as if he meant to defend his choice before a public audience, we would say that he protests *too much*, interpreting his zeal as a sign of confusion or insecurity. Being overly anxious to justify his beloved, he might foolishly deny various facts about her which a healthy relationship could admit and reduce to insignificance. Or he might exaggerate her virtues. In either case the fault lies not with the personal relationship through which he regards his beloved, but with the underlying assumption that he owes himself or his detractors an objectively compelling argument for his choice. That assumption is really what is unreasonable here; the confused lover invokes an inappropriate model of reasonable judgment. He thinks that he is being more reasonable than those who have no compelling grounds to offer for their loves, but in fact the joke is on him.

The logical contours of faith, particularly in this last respect, resemble those of love. The requirements of reasonable judgment shift when matters of faith confront us, just as they do when affairs of the heart command our attention. Since one needs a working understanding of religious principles to grasp their point and to feel their force, one cannot resolve his doubts about them without personal familiarity. Some religious claims, like some potential lovers, we can rule out without ever taking them to heart. We can rule them out wherever we have telling grounds against them; i.e., when we know that they are dependent on historical or scientific falsehoods, when they are logically inconsistent or incoherent, or when they entail morally unacceptable implications. Yet some religious teachings will survive this kind of screening, and if we are ever to believe that some of these remaining beliefs are true, we will have to enter into a working relationship with them. That is why we all begin with what is proximate, in religion as in love. Some more worldly experience may be desirable in both cases; yet no matter how broad our horizons, we still have to start with what, or whom, we know well enough to appreciate. The same asymmetry which confines the judgment of the lover to familiar persons, therefore, also limits the judgment of the believers to those teachings whose point he fully understands. Other options he need not denounce until and unless he knows them well enough to appreciate their force and to judge their compatibility.

Those who think that religious belief must be irrational if it is blind, then, are correct, but they usually misunderstand the cause of this blindness. Such critics take it for granted that the prospective believer must leap blindly and arbitrarily into a religion if he has no telling grounds on which to base his selection. Yet the attempt to provide such grounds no more solves this difficulty than the attempt to provide the prospective lover with objective criteria for choosing a mate solves his difficulty. In both cases the true cause of blindness comes from presumptuous and premature judgment, whereby we weigh our options without a duly appreciative understanding of what we have before us. The doctrine of predestination sounds unjust, the doctrine of the trinity sounds inconsistent, the doctrine of the reincarnation of unreal selves sounds incoherent; and so we reject them all. This is as it should be if these initial judgments are correct; but if they are passed without any understanding of the point of these doctrines, then the skeptic who rejects them on the basis of his superficial impressions and in the name of reason runs the same risk that the lover does when he rejects a would-be mate who seems at first unattractive. Just as the rejected lover may have hidden charms, such beliefs may have hidden forcefulness and sense, something which emerges only in the context of a closer working relationship. That kind of relationship reveals the point of believing and thereby clarifies *what* these murky doctrines actually mean to say. So once the point of a principle (its logical role) is understood, one can see how deceptive appearances can be. What appears to be a harsh, inconsistent, or incoherent teaching may prove to be quite the reverse. Of course, this might *not* happen, too. But in matters of faith, where principles are at issue, such a closer, personal, look is the *only* cure for blindness.

This does not mean that one has to become a believer before he can understand religious claims. Many people undoubtedly do profess beliefs which they do not completely understand, just as many people marry others whom they do not really know. This, however, is certainly not a requirement of reasonable belief. The important thing is to understand religious teachings well enough to know what their adoption would involve — what it would mean to conform to them, to bring one's thinking into line with them, to rely on them as a foundation of judgment, and to dispose one's life accordingly. One can have this kind of understanding without being committed to religious principles, or without even having any confidence in them at all; but one cannot acquire such confidence or commitment without *eventually* resting the weight of his thinking on them. The believer, like the lover, ventures his confidence in the hope that it will be sustained. If it is, if he finds these beliefs to be capacitating, then he can afford to strengthen his commitment.

If this still seems too fideistic, perhaps we should exploit the love analogy even further. Suppose someone has no working knowledge of any religious principles or of any comparable truths to live by. Suppose he is simply lost in the midst of life's perplexities and apparent senselessness, like a person who feels lost and alone without someone to love. Such a person, if he wants to proceed rationally, needs to cultivate some relationships, not so much with people as with teachings. If he does not know where to start, he might as well start with that which seems initially admirable, appealing, and suited to his sensibilities. In the case of love we know pretty well what this means, and we approve of it, even though we know that such initial infatuation is not love. In the case of religious belief, the initially attractive features of a religion may be harder to describe, but they are nonetheless desirable and appropriate. Some religions may seem more admirable than others because of the richer conceptions of fulfillment which they involve, or because of the nobler virtues which they call forth. Some may seem more appealing because of the moral teachings and the practical life which accompany them. Some may seem more suitable because they speak more directly to the potential believer's despair. It would be very foolish to discount these factors in the generation of religious belief. They are just the sort of thing which insures it against arbitrariness. They give the believer something to go by in searching for the conceptual means of addressing his concerns in a new order of judgment. Yet in faith, as in love, these initially attractive features must eventually give way to the overriding test of reliability, whereby the capacitating or incapacitating effect of religious principles eliminates or exacerbates the need for further justification.

Yet what if one feels no *need* to "make sense" out of life in the first place? Obviously, if one has yet to struggle with the concerns and perplexities which religious beliefs address, no *argument* is likely to move him toward faith. An argument might compel a dispassionate form of assent, and then we might expect an emotional overlay of commitment to follow; but this makes about as much sense as the expectation that passionate love will develop in a marriage which has been "rationally" arranged by a computer. Of course that *might* happen, but it is not a reliable expectation. Both faith and love are conditioned by sensitivities which must be present and engaged if either is to develop. The lover may need to know something of loneliness and empty relationships to appreciate a partner as a potential mate, and the believer may need to know something of life's transiency and sorrow to appreciate the higher teleology of a religious outlook. The lover only learns what his beloved *means* to him against a background of mature experience, and so too the believer. Only when he has the requisite sensitivity to be troubled by religious concerns, by the apparent absurdity of his fate, the futility of his striving, or the evil within and without—only then may he be in a position to appreciate what it would mean to submit his troubled thoughts to the new ordering of a religious set of principles. Then, though, his growing attraction to such teachings ceases to be arbitrary or blind. It beomes conditioned by the only factors that could ever engender full understanding and reasonable conviction.

The importance of "due maturity," as Luther put it, is so great that the attempt to persuade someone to accept religious principles often consists of little more than the attempt to evoke the necessary concerns. Just as loneliness ripens the heart and gives the unsteady lover a new regard for an old acquaintance, the weight of spiritual concerns deepens the potential believer's appreciation for teachings which otherwise seem like naive superstitions. This quickens the believer's understanding, enlivening the options by driving home their point. Accordingly, Christian apologetics often begin with a discussion of sin; once the seriousness of the problem is clear, the proferred solution carries more force. That is also why moral persuasion, or the advocacy of any other fundamental principles, typically begins with the cultivation of the difficulties which they address. One wants to show that there are aspects of our experience which cry out for some means of disciplined comprehension, aspects which might be conceptually managed in judgment if only we had the necessary principles to guide our thinking. This is not a gimmick; it is an essential part of rational persuasion when principles are at stake.

Put in summary fashion like this, the necessity of beginning with live options in matters of faith may seem too obvious to belabor. Yet this simple truth belies a dimension of religious belief which is altogether lacking in the usual pseudorationalistic conception of religious conviction. It is all too easy, especially in an academic context, to suppose that a reasonable believer must study the world's great religions and array them all before him as alternatives from which a selection is to be made. Not only is this an artificial conception of religious belief in the first place, it also leads to the completely gratuitous assumption that there must be adequate criteria for making such a selection. Without such telling criteria, we seem forced to admit the arbitrary subjectivity of religious belief. So we insist on having these criteria, and we dismiss those philosophies of religion which do not provide them. By what logical right do we do this? The only semi-plausible answer is that rational beliefs are always, of necessity, dependent on some objective standards for their justification. But this, as we have already seen, is not the case. In matters of principle, reason requires that we begin with teachings whose point and force we appreciate and understand. Instead of choosing impartially from a host of alternatives, arranged as competing hypotheses, we begin with our liveliest options, the ones to which we are already partial—and then we use objective criteria to *restrain* our convictions, not to generate them.

To put all this in another way, we *underestimate* what it takes to bring religious teachings to life as serious options. It is not enough to understand the words employed in the formulation of various beliefs, since the regulatory role that these beliefs play as principles adds another dimension to their sense. That aspect of their sense cannot always be picked up with a little further academic study. It presumes something in the way of personal development, so that the underlying sensitivities and concerns can nurture the potential believer's appreciation of the point of the principles which he is offered. Until one has this kind of understanding, he is in no position to compare and contrast possible alternatives. Simply ranging various teachings against some generally applicable standards such as coherence and consistency does not bring these options to life. It simply makes believing a premature and empty exercise.

To take religious teachings seriously and to judge them appropriately, one must concentrate his interest in a more or less exclusive manner, centering his thoughts on those whose point and promise he understands. One might have a working understanding of more than one religion, just as one might be intimate with more than one lover. Yet one still has to "test" his principles by following them, much as a lover must test his love by relying on it. Then, if the believer finds that the principles which he chooses hold up, that they enable him to reduce more and more of the anomalies of his experience to some sort of ordered understanding, he may be able to dismiss his other live options as incompatible possibilities. His dead options, those whose point he never understood, will remain outside the proper scope of his judgments. Thus the built-in exclusivity of religious commitment does not come about as the result of choosing one option and ruling out all the others in the same series of comparative tests. It comes from having to limit one's thinking to those beliefs which one can understand well enough to judge in practice.

2

The only trouble with this analogy between faith and love is that the lover only has to decide what is right *for him*, whereas the believer needs to determine what is right *for anyone*. In affirming his principles as *truths*, the believer holds his beliefs for any and all persons, but the lover never supposes that everyone else should choose one and the same person to love. Thus, if we liken the "truth" of the believer's convictions to the "rightness" of the lover's choice, we may find it hard to resist a purely subjective account of faith. What is "true" for one person may not be "true" for another. Yet if we insist that truth is at stake in matters of faith, and that error is a possibility, then we may have to give up the analogy between faith and love.

In defense of the analogy, it may be said that matters of the heart are not entirely subjective. Love, at least, is not self-certifying. When it is tempted and begins to fade, the troubled lover cannot always allay his doubts simply by strengthening his commitment. As he knows very well, he can have made a poor choice. Merely thinking that he has made the right one does not make it so. Nevertheless, the fact remains that the lover's judgments are qualified by the need to determine only what is right for him, whereas the believer's judgments, being truth claims, represent unqualified claims about what is the case and ought (ideally) to be believed by anyone. Here the analogy does break down, but we do not have to revoke anything we have said so far about the asymmetry of religious conviction to acknowledge this difference. We simply need to supplement the analogy with some further analysis.

Presumably, to believe that one's own religion is true, one must believe that every other religion is false. Since this is the objection which seems to destroy the analogy between love and faith, this is the assumption which must be challenged. It may seem safe enough at first, but it turns out to be far more debatable than one might think. For one thing, it is not clear just what the source of such exclusivity is supposed to be. This exclusivity could be ascribed to the peculiar demands of *religious* conviction, or it could be attributed to the *generic* features of belief. The first alternative is highly dubious, since the devotees of some religions make it a point of faith to repudiate other religions, while other believers explicitly hold out a place for the truth contained in other religions. In the Athanasian Creed, for example, one finds the Christian faith proclaimed as the only true faith. In Hinduism, by contrast, one finds the view that all great religions share in the one truth which includes all partial truths and all particular faiths. Here there is no *avowed* exclusivity, and so it obviously will not do to say that religious belief is bound to be exclusive because every religion teaches the falsity of every other religion. Religions differ on this point.

Yet even if every religion did include explicit denunciations of other faiths, individual believers would not have to share in these denunciations. To suppose that they could not be Christians, for example, without endorsing the rejection of other religions would be to confuse religious belief with party affiliation. Becoming religious is primarily a matter of having one's thoughts and one's passions informed by a new set of concepts and principles, not a matter of joining one particular group in preference to another. Religious organizations are undoubtedly necessary to preserve and to nurture religious understanding, and these organizations may very well need to define themselves in contrast to one another. The believer who best exemplifies and upholds his traditions, however, is not the one who has a passion for religious institutions but the one who keeps his moral struggles and his existential concerns in the perspective afforded by his principles. Most believers, in fact, do not even know all the official dogmas of their churches or their traditions, and many do not understand some of the teachings which they do know. So if one had to understand and to accept all the doctrines of a religion to be a believer, few ordinary believers would qualify.

The point here is not to criticize institutional religion but to show that the exclusiveness which religions accrue theologically in their institutionalized forms is not entailed by the nature of *faith.* Party disputes in religious matters are bound to arise, and the history of religion is to a large extent a history of perpetual disagreement and conflict. Yet one can be religious *without taking sides on every issue.* The idea that one must affiliate with a particular religious party to become a religious believer rests on the mistaken idea that we must compare and contrast whole sets of doctrines if we are to affirm any religious teachings. We do not have to do that — indeed, we cannot do that without treating religious principles as hypotheses and thereby obscuring their point. The understanding we need comes from the intensification of possibilities, not from their multiplication. We need depth more than breadth to avoid prejudging religious principles. Thus we do not have to develop every potential contrast between our beliefs and the beliefs of others. Battles enough are already raging, and new ones can doubtlessly be joined; but the would-be believer does not have to fight them all to conform his thoughts to religious ideals.

In view of the widespread antipathy toward all forms of exclusiveness, and in view of the debilitating relativism which usually accompanies this antipathy, the last point seems well worth emphasizing. One does not have to be a relativist to avoid presumptuous denials of other religions; one need only give up the false ideal of comparing every religious claim with all its rivals, for we have no adequate list of independent criteria by which to judge them. Faith develops by fulfilling a (cognitive) *need*, not by fulfilling an abstract list of rational criteria.

Nevertheless, sooner or later we have to face the more serious objection that the exclusivity of religious belief belongs to the *generic* features of belief. The believer who does not want to adopt a negative stance toward other religious teachings cannot avoid doing so as long as he wishes to affirm his beliefs as truth claims. Elementary logic tells us that the affirmation of a proposition is equivalent to the denial of its contradictory, and this is such a rudimentary point of logic that we cannot abandon it without passing beyond the logic of truth claims altogether. As long as we continue to advance and espouse our religious beliefs as truth claims, how can we avoid the implicit denial of other religious claims? Clearly there must be *some* exclusivity built into religious belief, since believing that those who do not agree with us are *wrong* is simply the other side of affirming the *truth* of our own convictions. In this respect Hindus are no more tolerant than the most militant Christians, for a Hindu cannot affirm his own inclusive conception of faith without at the same time denying every other incompatible point of view. To all those who say, for example, that there is only one means of salvation, Hindus must say (or at least think), "you are wrong, there are many roads to the mountaintop." This is not inconsistency on their part; it is a logical necessity.

One cannot affirm a truth claim of any sort without denying every other incompatible assertion, whether one means to or not. This applies to religious assertions as well as to any other assertions. In fact, it is one of the strongest reasons we have for thinking that religious beliefs are truth claims. Religious believers refuse to admit the contradictories of what they say, something which they need not do if they are not asserting truth claims. Yet this elementary observation about truth claims is not as telling as it seems; for despite appearances, the doctrines of two different religions may be compatible (or even equivalent) in meaning, in which case the affirmation of one will obviously not entail a denial of the other. In other cases, religious claims will conflict; and then the believer who wishes to affirm one *will* have to deny the other once he sees their incompatibility. These two possibilities, however, do not exhaust the alternatives. There is a third possibility which is much more interesting. Instead of being compatible or incompatible, two different religious principles may stand in an indeterminate logical relationship, in which case the implicit exclusivity of religious belief becomes impossible to trace.

Instances of this third sort are more numerous than one might think. As missionaries come across various native beliefs, for example, they must often find themselves unable to say whether these native beliefs are compatible with their own. Admittedly, they may be uncertain because they do not understand the native beliefs well enough, or because they do not understand their own beliefs well enough. Yet the same uncertainty might also arise because the beliefs in question are too ill-defined to permit any *definitive* pronouncement. The concepts which they involve may have an "open texture," a sense which is clear enough for normal usages but not sufficiently clear for cross-cultural comparisons.

Consider miracle claims, for example. David Hume thought that the miracle stories of different religions mutually contradicted one another, so that a believer who accepted the miracle claims of his own tradition was thereby bound to reject those of another. Perhaps he assumed too much. Must a Christian deny every faith healing not conducted in the name of Christ? Must he ascribe such healings to the work of the devil, or must he turn to some psychological explanation? Does he know that God never intervenes in other contexts, perhaps even on other planets? Christian teachings just are not that clear, so there may not be an answer to be *discovered* at all. Instead of discovering the compatibility or incompatibility of certain miracle claims, believers may have to make a *ruling* on this point, thereby sharpening the sense of the claims which they wish to make. Prior to such rulings, the question of the compatibility of two religious assertions may be indeterminable. Indeed, why else should theologians have to *add* various teachings about what is to count as a miracle? — Only because on this and on other points of doctrine religions can be initially too ill-defined to settle the full range of their compatibility and incompatibility.

Perhaps it is the responsibility of theologians to clarify continually the teachings of their own traditions vis-a-vis those of other traditions. Certainly it is the responsibility of people engaged in the comparative study of religion, but that is not the point. The point is that these comparisons are bound to be difficult owing to the under-determination of the beliefs and concepts involved. The would-be *believer*, however, does not have to resolve these questions in order to adopt some religious principles. And to that extent he need not *presumptuously* deny every other religious claim.

One can easily become confused about this. Almost irresistibly the law of excluded middle tempts us to say that there cannot be indeterminate logical relationships between propositions. Either something is the case or it is not the case; this much seems certain, and so we have only to apply this law of logic to conclude of any two beliefs that they are either compatible or incompatible. Yet there is, in fact, another possibility, since the law of excluded middle does not *always* apply. In effect, this law says that we cannot simultaneously ascribe and deny a predicate to the same subject (e.g., that we cannot say of any two propositions that they are compatible and incompatible at the same time). With some subjects and some predicates, however, we cannot make any ascriptions *or* denials. This can happen for any one of several reasons: 1) because any use of the predicate would involve a "category mistake" (Arthur is either metrical or nonmetrical), (2) because the standards for applying the predicate are unclear (Arthur is either great or not great), or (3) because the subject itself is not sufficiently defined or developed to permit a confident judgment (young Arthur is a saint).

Although it is a bit more complicated, the attempt to compare two religious beliefs may run into difficulties of the third variety: the beliefs themselves and hence the relationship between them may be insufficiently developed to permit a confident judgment of their compatibility. They may be like two adolescents whose parents are trying to arrange a marriage — are the adolescents suited to each other or not? There may not be any answer to this question, not because the parents do not know their children well enough but because their children have not yet assumed sufficiently definite personalities. I see no reason why the same thing may not *at times* be said of religious beliefs. They too may not have assumed fully definite senses, so that comparative judgments might have to be postponed.

The only serious objection to this would be to argue that truth claims must always have fully determinate senses, so that propositions which can be said to be true or false must also be definitely compatible or incompatible. This objection, however, sounds more powerful than it is. It makes more sense if hypotheses are being compared than it does if principles are being examined, for the meaning of hypotheses is more determinate than the meaning of principles. Inasmuch as hypotheses have independently specifiable truth conditions, the meanings of an obscure hypothesis can be spelled out in a more definitive way by being restated in terms of these conditions. What it would take to confirm a hypothesis tells us, in effect, what it would mean for it to be true. Consequently, the same thing which makes an assertion a hypothesis — i.e., independent truth conditions — also makes it comparable to other hypotheses. The data needed to confirm two different hypotheses provide the means of determining their compatibility or incompatibility. Indeed, the positivists could have (and perhaps should have) advanced their verification principle as a means of showing when two ostensibly different hypotheses are actually equivalent in meaning. If these hypotheses have the same truth conditions, then they have the same meaning. Alternatively, if they have incompatible truth conditions, then they are genuine rivals.

Principles, however, have no independently specifiable truth conditions, and therefore they cannot be so *definitively* compared and contrasted in terms of what it would take to verify or falsify them. At least they do not have the kind of truth conditions which would enable their sense to be explained in terms of the evidence needed to confirm them. If one wants to know exactly what a principle *says* as a truth claim, he must study the kind of judgments which follow from it. This may seem like an odd way of clarifying the sense of an assertion, but if fundamental principles say what they say about the world by saying what sort of judgments our experience calls for, then nothing could be more appropriate. We see what a principle means by seeing *how it informs further judgment.* This applies to the belief in nature's uniformity, to the belief in free will, to the belief in God, and to every other indemonstrable principle. To say that human beings have free will, for example, is not to say that they have any property which might be discovered in inspection, or which might show itself indirectly through symptoms of its presence. It is to say that a vast range of human behavior needs to be understood and evaluated in terms of motives, reasons, rationales, responsibilities, and so on. These orders of judgment do not follow from evidence which can be independently discovered in human physiology or human behavior. Rather, they tell us what it *means* to talk of free will and what it means to believe in it.

That is why the mastery of true principles represents only what one might call a "working knowledge" of the world, a knowledge which is adequate for the purpose of advancing fruitful forms of inquiry but which cannot be translated into a specified list of confirmed facts. One who has mastered a principle cannot explain what he knows in terms of mere information. He has to impart the concepts and capacities which are required to bring a certain range of experience under the canopy of a disciplined form of thinking. Here there is no short-cut to understanding. Both the force *and the sense* of fundamental principles reside in this kind of working knowledge.

The comparison of religious principles, therefore, is bound to be difficult. Instead of clarifying the implications of these principles by describing the states of affairs which would have to obtain for them to be true, one needs to elucidate the point of these beliefs before he can usefully compare them. One must understand above all else the role which they are intended to play in the regulation of a believer's thought. This does not mean that we will never be able to say that various religious claims are incompatible, but it does mean that one needs to know how two principles compete in proposing different patterns of interpretation or explanation for the same aspects of experience before he can say that they are definitely incompatible. One may not understand difficult beliefs, such as the doctrine of predestination, well enough to do this. Or the point of various beliefs may be so obscure, ambiguous, or undeveloped that one could not compare it to other beliefs with any confidence or success even if he wanted to. If one could resort to comparisons based on independently specifiable truth conditions, many of these problems could be overcome; but the lack of such conditions in principles makes their senses doubly difficult to establish and compare — difficult, at times, even to the point of impossibility.

Once again, however, the potential believer does not have to sort out all these ill-defined relationships to address questions of faith in a reasonable way. He does not have to know the full range of compatibility or incompatibility between the doctrines of one religion and those of another. The only kind of understanding which reason requires in matters of faith is an understanding of what it would mean to conform his thinking and practice to a few basic principles. He need not even understand all of the teachings which belong to the same family of beliefs. For the believer, like the lover, can deal responsibly only with his live options, and all the teachings of a religion do not come alive at once. They come alive in stages as one learns to understand and appreciate their point. No matter how much one's understanding grows, it will not and need not include every religious belief from every religion. Some dead options will remain, and the reasonable believer will not have to pass judgment upon them. Confining himself instead to his live options, he will have to rest the weight of his thinking on them. Only when he is disappointed and still unable to make any teleological sense out of his experience will he need to turn away from those beliefs whose point he does not understand, toward those whose point and force he has yet to grasp.

In a logical as well as in a practical sense, then, we can still say what we set out to say. We cannot expect a potential believer to set out a vast array of religious beliefs as competing hypotheses. We can expect him (ideally) to avoid inconsistency; and to that extent we can expect him to reject any beliefs which are incompatible with his own. That is part of what it means to affirm the *truth* of beliefs, and it would be foolish to surrender this requirement in the name of greater tolerance. The only thing which the believer needs to give up is presumptuousness in repudiating other religious principles. He need not presume that religious beliefs whose point he does not understand *must* be incompatible with his own beliefs, simply because they are different. Nor does he need to undertake comparisons to justify his own convictions or to deal responsibly with his doubts. In some cases, a believer might sharpen his own beliefs by defining them vis-a-vis various alternatives. In other cases, such comparisons might show the believer that he has far more in common with other believers than he thought. So we should reserve an important place for comparative studies of religion, but we should not require these studies of all those who wish to commit themselves to religious principles. A reasonable faith requires the deepening of one's understanding before it requires broadening through comparisons.

We need to remember this lest we straddle ourselves with a dangerously false picture of reasonable religious belief. We need not affirm a religious principle by denying every apparent alternative, because we need not and should not attempt to judge them as competing hypotheses. The logical status of religious principles requires another approach, one in which dimly understood and ill-defined alternatives may simply be ignored.

In arguing for the possibility of this sort of benign neglect in matters of faith, I am not trying to encourage or discourage an inclusive acceptance of other religions. I do not know how far the world's religions are compatible, and I do not think that there is any straightforward way to find out. A purely logical analysis of the nature of faith claims cannot tell us that, but it can tell us that a presumptuous dogmatism born of treating religious beliefs as competing hypotheses and a commodious relativism born of noncognitivist accounts of faith are both wrong. Finally, it can tell us not to worry over securing our beliefs against every other belief. The doubts which arise from the sheer presence of other religions can only be resolved in a manner appropriate to principles. One must allow the weight of his thinking to rest upon his principles by degrees, until the fear that they have no truth has been replaced by the capacities which hold them in place and the demand for stronger forms of justification has subsided.

NOTES

1. From Johannes Colerus in the introduction to *The Chief Works of Benedict de Spinoza*, trans. R. H. M. Elwes (New York: Dover, 1951), vol. I, xix.

2. Spinoza, *Theological-Political Treaties*, in *Chief Works*, vol. I, 9-10 *passim.*

3. *Ibid.*, pp. 186-187. Spinoza could not have regarded these seven dogmas as pseudo-assertions, since several of them — e.g., the claim that God is one — coincide with the metaphysical propositions of the *Ethics*. At best one might say that Spinoza thought that each believer was free to interpret these dogmas in the way most conducive to piety *for him*, but the fact remains that Spinoza drew the line against complete relativism here.

4. Søren Kierkegaard, *The Journals of Søren Kierkegaard*, trans. Alexander Dru (Oxford: Oxford University Press, 1938), entry number 922.

WORKS CITED

Ayer, Alfred Jules. *Language, Truth and Logic*. New York: Dover Publications, 1952.

Edwards, Paul, ed. *The Encyclopedia of Philosophy*. New York: MacMillan, 1967.

Flew, Antony, and Alasdair MacIntyre. *New Essays in Philosophical Theology*. New York: MacMillan, 1955.

Hudson, W. D. *Wittgenstein and Religious Belief*. London: MacMillan, 1975.

James, William. *Pragmatism*. New York: Longmans, Green, and Co., 1907.

_____. *The Varieties of Religious Experience*. New York: Longmans, Green, and Co., 1902.

_____. *The Will to Believe*. New York: Longmans, Greens, and Co., 1898.

Kierkegaard, Søren. *The Journals of Søren Kierkegaard*. Edited by Alexander Dru. Oxford: Oxford University Press, 1938.

Luther, Martin. *Martin Luther*. Edited by John Dillenberger. Garden City: Anchor Books, 1961.

Moore, G. E. *Philosophical Papers*. New York: MacMillan, 1949.

Morawetz, Thomas. *Wittgenstein and Knowledge*. Amherst: University of Massachusetts Press, 1978.

Spinoza, Benedict de. *The Chief Works of Benedict de Spinoza*. Edited by R. H. M. Elwes. New York: Dover, 1951.

Wittgenstein, Ludwig. *Lectures and Conversations on Aesthetics, Psychology, and Religious Belief*. Edited by Cyril Barrett. Berkeley: University of California Press, 1967.

_____. *On Certainty*. New York: J. J. Harper, 1969.

_____. *Tractatus Logico-Philosophicus*. London: Routledge and Kegan Paul, Ltd., 1961.

ABOUT THE AUTHOR

John H. Whittaker is a member of the Department of Philosophy and Religious Studies and Director of the Program in Religious Studies at Louisiana State University. He has previously taught at the University of Virginia and Quinnipiac College. Professor Whittaker holds the B.A. degree from Pomona College, the M.A.R. degree from Yale Divinity School, and the M. Phil. and Ph.D. degrees from Yale University. He has published numerous articles and reviews in scholarly journals and has presented papers at meetings of the American Academy of Religion, the Society for the Philosophy of Religion, and the Society for Religion in Higher Education. He has been guest lecturer at the Boston University Institute for Philosophy and Religion and at various colleges and universities. Professor Whittaker is presently at work on a small volume entitled *Admiration and Persuasion*, and on another book, *Reductive Accounts of Religious Belief.*